relat

MOVING ON

relate
MOVING ON

Breaking up without breaking down

Suzie Hayman

Vermilion
LONDON

Text © Suzie Hayman and Relate 2001

Suzie Hayman has asserted her right to be identified as the author of this work under the Copyright, Designs and Patent Act 1988.

First published in the United Kingdom in 2001 by Vermilion
an imprint of Ebury Press
Random House, 20 Vauxhall Bridge Road, London SW1V 2SA

Random House Australia Pty Limited
20 Alfred Street, Milsons Point, Sydney,
New South Wales 2061, Australia

Random House New Zealand Limited
18 Poland Road, Glenfield,
Auckland 10, New Zealand

Random House (Pty) Limited
Isle of Houghton, Corner of Boundary Road & Carse O'Gowrie
Houghton 2198, South Africa

Random House Publishers India Private Limited
301 World Trade Tower, Hotel Intercontinental Grand Complex,
Barakhamba Lane, New Delhi 110 001, India

The Random House Group Limited Reg. No. 954009

A CIP catalogue record for this book is available from the British Library

ISBN 9780091856250
ISBN 0091856256

Printed and bound in Great Britain by
Mackays of Chatham plc, Chatham, Kent

Papers used by Vermilion are natural, recyclable products made from wood grown in sustainable forests.

CONTENTS

ACKNOWLEDGEMENTS

With gratitude and acknowledgements to the counsellors, clients and readers who contributed their stories, questions and suggestions. Thanks also to past and present members of Relate – Sue Broome, Norma Heaton, Derek Hill, Suzy Powling, Marj Thoburn and Angela Sibson. I am also particularly indebted to Joanna Carreras and Jacqueline Korn for their support, patience and help.

INTRODUCTION

Nothing is forever. Fairy stories and Hollywood films want you to believe that the story finishes with a wedding or when the happy couple ride off into the sunset. And that once that happens, nothing more of note will occur. Once boy and girl have got together, we are persuaded that their idyll will continue, unchanged and undisturbed. The conclusion most of us come to is that once we have our relationship, there is and should be a 'Happily Ever After' for all of us. In the real world, we sadly discover that it isn't quite like that. Virtually everyone, at sometime or another in their lives, has to face up to the ending of a relationship. This is a hurtful and difficult experience, whether the twosome was one that had lasted ten weeks or ten years and whether the other person finished it or you dumped them. Endings happen, and if you've invested time, effort, emotion and a little bit of yourself into being with another person, when there is a parting there will be pain. Dealing with the pain is often made that much more difficult by the belief that it shouldn't be happening and that, if it is, we must be uniquely incompetent or singularly bad people to have allowed this to happen.

Loss and separation are nothing new. Whenever it was that our ancestors first invented pair bonding – whether they were still in the trees or had just moved into caves – the fact is that shortly after finding the joys of being together, someone would have discovered the agony of losing their other half. However, over much of human history the parting of the ways for a couple tended to be when death did them part. In most cultures, marriage was for life, and marriage was felt to be the only social arrangement that made a sexual relationship respectable. 'For life', however, didn't mean what it does today. The average life expectancy at the beginning of this century was late forties for men and early fifties for women, and was an even younger age in earlier times. Coupled with late marriage that meant that the average union probably lasted less than twenty years. Today, even twenty years of marriage still leaves you with a major part of your life to lead. For more and more people the reality of modern life is that one person, one love, one relationship or marriage is not going to see you through from the beginning of your sexual life to the day you die. Quite apart from anything else, many of us now start off our sexual lives with permanency the last thing on our minds. The average age for first intercourse is seventeen while the average age on a first marriage is 30 for men and almost 28 for women. Twenty-five per cent of us have had intercourse before the age of sixteen and the vast majority by the time we're twenty. While some people are celibate in the gap years between sexual maturity and eventually finding the perfect mate, and some do marry early, most play the field in their teens and twenties knowing this time it's not for ever. It's only as we approach and enter late twenties and thirties that most people do make relationships which we hope will last. Sadly, a large number of us watch them break up sooner or later. According to the latest figures, two in five marriages end in divorce and we have no figures for the number of long-term relationships that end in painful separation. By 2010 it is predicted that cohabitation, marriage, divorce and remarriage will be the normal pattern of family formation. It may not be easy to recognise we're in the middle of a social trend, but we are. Make no mistake – it's already here.

But while more and more people are having to cope with

break-up, we seem to be no better at dealing with the situation. Endings are always difficult and it can be enormously hard to let go, either of the other person, the relationship or the feelings of anger, guilt or despair brought on by the break up. Depression, anger, lack of self-esteem and feelings of failure are all common responses to the break-up of a relationship. Whether a partnership has lasted twelve months or twenty years, whether it was with or without 'benefit of clergy', realising that a parting of the ways is approaching can be the signal for misery, hostility and even violence. Couples and individuals can frequently become 'stuck', unable to move beyond their anger or pain. A break-up so often leads to a break down, as everyone involved struggles with destructive emotions, and becomes bogged down in destructive behaviour.

This is true equally for a couple who only have themselves to consider, as it is for a couple with children. When there are children involved, however, the couple have the added complexity of having to cope not only with their own emotions but the confusion and upset of others too. According to the latest statistics, three in five divorcing couples have children under the age of sixteen, which is why it is estimated that 28 per cent of children will experience their parents' divorce before the age of sixteen. Official statistics don't count how many cohabiting parents separate, so the figures for children seeing their family disintegrate about them is actually even higher.

Young people exhibit a variety of reactions to the upheaval of family change. Some withdraw into silence, moodiness or truculence. Some show open anger, with destructive impulses directed outward to others or inwards to themselves, in risk-taking or anti-social behaviour. Some express guilt and distress and blame themselves, others vent their feelings on other people, often at the members of their family they feel will stand by them. Young people who are members of a separated family are more likely to truant, leave school early, get fewer qualifications, experiment with sex early, marry early and have children early. But often their behaviour, which is a cry of protest and pain at what is happening around them, is misunderstood by parents and professionals. As an agony aunt I get many letters that complain about children being out of control and delinquent, and add as an after-thought 'I've got enough on my plate at the moment as our relationship is going through a bad patch', as if the two events have no link whatsoever. As Peter Wilson, Director of the children's charity *Young Minds*, that helps parents who are worried about their children's emotional wellbeing, has said: 'What it means is that you're getting a lot of children labelled as bad kids or difficult kids and what they really are is sad kids.'

But some couples and some families pass through the experience of separation and/or divorce, with all its potential for damage, and emerge confident, happy and whole. What turns divorce and separation from a disaster into just another passage of life that can be met? Some people, while not exactly sailing through it, do at least appear able to cope with what others find devastating and overwhelming. All the evidence suggests that it is how you manage change that matters, not the fact that you experience such a change in your life. You may have thought that it's all the luck of the draw. Whether you go under or manage to deal with such a difficult situation isn't all down to fate, innate character or your stars. It's my firm belief that how you deal with setbacks in life has everything to do with the lessons you learn as you grow up. There are reasons for why you may find a break-up particularly difficult and what could make it more bearable. Once you understand the buttons that are pushed in you that hold you back, you can set about managing change to make it easier. This book will help you identify your particular trigger points – the particular events or emotions that hurt or make you feel overwhelmed – and so aid you in getting on top and in control.

This may be especially important in relationships that are violent or abusive, physically or emotionally, or turn ugly when one partner declares the intention to leave.

The aim of this book will be to help you acquire the skills to deal with break-up confidently, competently and well. I intend to offer insights and explanations, suggestions and ideas to help you and your family face up to the ending of a relationship. We will examine how we, as adults, feel and act when our relationships crumble, and how we might approach the event in as constructive a manner as possible. We will explore how children may see a break-up – their fears, fantasies and hopes – and how adults may help them cope with the inevitable. If we could understand our own feelings and those of any young people involved in such a difficult event, and offer support, rather than being overcome by our own concerns or casting blame, the painful experience of seeing your family separate would be more manageable. What is most important for any child is that their parents may stop being a couple but can never opt out from being a parent. The emphasis throughout the book will be on managing the change, on being honest but tactful, sympathetic but firm. The overall aim will be to look at how family break down and re-partnering affects children, and how best we can manage such events.

For those who are not parents, it may seem that making an ending should be simpler. You may kick against accepting that your relationship is over, you may be the one to skip off into the sunset, glad to be free. Whichever, once you have separated, there may only be memories to hold you together. Those people who have left a relationship because of unhappiness or even abuse, or who experienced a particularly bitter parting, may be tempted to wipe out even memories and consign this relationship to the trash can – out of sight, out of mind and out of your life for good. But it is important to recognise that even a bad relationship has something important to teach us. Indeed, such an experience is part of your life and so part of your history and personality. Trying to delete it deletes an important part of yourself. Probably the most important task when a relationship finishes is to make a distinction between ending and erasing. When you make a good ending, you don't do it by wiping out a person or a part of your past. You do it by embracing what has gone before, having closure and moving on. It would be far better to accept and celebrate the good bits and accept and learn from the bad. Remember, those who do not learn from the past are doomed to repeat it.

But before we look at how to deal with endings we need to explore just exactly why the skills may be hard to acquire and difficult to apply. The challenge is to move on – to be able to accept the breaking up of a relationship without letting it destroy you. Part of that process is to let yourself experience the sad, angry, desperate feelings that losing something and someone you value will naturally give rise to. You can't put an ending properly behind you, indeed, until you have wept, screamed, argued and mourned. There is a way that we can view problems that can help us approach and work to finding an answer in unhappy relationships. It's called The 'Four Steps' rule. This is:

- Working out what's really wrong or what's making it difficult
- Getting the picture
- Working out what we want to do
- Doing something about it

'Working out what's really wrong' and 'Doing something about it' are probably the hardest of the four steps. We often think we know what is wrong, and just as frequently concentrate our complaints, bitterness or anger on a red herring. For instance, couples and individuals sometimes focus all their efforts on arguing money and law, when what they really need to discuss is feelings. You and a partner may have endless arguments about being untidy, being late, being inattentive when the real complaint should be 'I feel you don't love me and you don't value me'. Even once we are aware of the problem, and have worked out what's wrong, why it's happened, and what we would like to be different, actually putting it into practice can seem impossible. By helping you do the first step and face up to the other three, *Moving On – Breaking Up Without Breaking Down* will help you put the fourth, final piece of the jigsaw into place.

Chapter One

FACING UP TO ENDINGS

'When my marriage ended, I knew it would hurt, and hurt for some time. We'd been together eight years and I had thought we were going to be together for life. There were tears and moments of real, black despair when he left, but I did think it would get better after a time. Two years on, I was still paralysed by fear and depression. I couldn't believe how long it affected me, and how badly. I couldn't think straight, I couldn't do the simplest things. I just felt so useless and such a failure. And it wasn't because he'd dumped me. I was the one to say the marriage was over and throw him out, not the other way round. But it was as if I couldn't go anywhere from there. I couldn't believe it was really over and face up to life without him, for such a long time.'

When a relationship comes to an end, you would think there would be a moment when you'd realise it's over. Perhaps a day, an hour or a second, when you know the love you shared is gone and the relationship just isn't working. An objective bystander might be able to tell you that's the time to pack up and move on, but it's far easier said than done. Around 160,000 married couples untied the knot in the UK last year, and who knows how many called it a day after living together without going through a formal ceremony? Some may appear to have been able to shake hands and kiss cheeks at the farewell, wish each other good luck and pass on to a new life with a few regrets and only a little hurt. Many find the transition from being a couple to being alone again *devastating*. What most of us would like, when a relationship ends, is to make sense of what happened and why, and to cope with our feelings. In effect, we want to stand up after that knockdown fight, dust ourselves off and stride on. What so often happens is that we get stuck. The experience is so painful, so confusing, so overwhelming that we crumble. We can't move on and resume our lives. The break-up really breaks us up.

THE MYTHS

Myths often slow us down and hold us back from dealing with the tragedies in our lives. One is that men are somehow less romantic than women, looking for sex rather than love, and being quick to trade in an old partner for a younger model. Many people believe men get over a break-up more easily and even prefer the footloose, fancy-free life of a single person while women crave safety and security. Men can appear to confirm this, by rapidly losing touch with old partners and their own kids, while women seem to confirm their needy, dependant status by being quick to cry over and mourn a relationship that has come to an end. Seeing men as hard and strong, women as soft and weak may stop you understanding what has happened and why. It may prevent you seeking answers to how to deal with a break-up, and how to maintain links if you have a family. This book is about taking on the challenge of a relationship that is ending, and winning. Not winning in a battle with another person, but winning in the fight against despair and depression and all the feelings of failure and blame that we so often heap on our own heads when a relationship breaks down. The last thing you may need is someone standing back, lecturing you and trying to tell you how to cope with a broken relationship. What would be helpful, however, is some encouragement and a guide to marshalling the skills you already have, to help yourself make the very best of the rest of your life. This is what I hope you will find, in these pages.

In order to move on, it helps first to understand why we may find it so difficult to cope with breaking up. Well, that's easy, you might say. Having a relationship end is enough to knock anyone for six – isn't it? But there is more to it than just the shock and pain of having love turn cold on you; this particular love, at this particular time and in this particular fashion. Losing contact with people who mean something to you is always going to be painful. When a person or a relationship dies, you feel regrets and sorrow. When you part company with a person or group of people with whom you've spent time, as a couple, or in a group, at school, work or even on a short-term experience such as on holiday, you are bound to feel sad. But there are other losses that hurt in similar ways. Even coming to the end of a film, a day out or something as terminally trivial and short-lived as an ice cream, you are ending an experience which you have enjoyed and might wish would go on a bit longer. You might think that how you cope with and how you feel about the end of something has to do with its relative importance. So, you might assume you would feel a whole lot better about coming to the end of a stick of rock than you do with facing up to the end of a twenty-year marriage. As anyone who has gone through a traumatic period in their life can tell you however, sometimes it's the apparently little things that push you over the edge. Having coped with an admirably stiff upper lip to your house burning down, your partner leaving and the dog dying, you may be reduced to hysterical tears at breaking a tea cup. The truth is that how you deal with an ending, *any* ending and *all* endings, whether it's the end of a phone call or the end of twenty years of on-going friendship, are one and the same skills. Some people seem to go to pieces when they lose touch with someone they've known for a couple of weeks, or are terrible at drawing a line and ending a chat. Others can survive the loss of a parent, a partner, a child, and are always the ones to sign off and put down the phone. The difference between being the one who can withdraw and cope with an ending and the one who can't, is how you have learned to cope with endings, not the particular thing you are losing.

> **Endings are always hard**
> **There is no such thing as a Good Ending**

ENDINGS ARE ALWAYS HARD

Many of us, when forced to deal with a parting, assume that how we are coping – or not coping – is to do with the relationship, the other person or our own inadequacies. We may focus on the here and now, and assume that this is where the problem lies. We may blame the partnership, assuming that it was doomed from the beginning and saying we never should have settled down and trusted it. We may blame the other person, and become convinced that they were evil, vicious, cheating and cruel and were so from the beginning, if only we'd realised. More often, we blame ourselves and beat ourselves up for being failures, neither attractive nor worthwhile enough to have kept the other person interested, and for not deserving to be loved. What we often fail to realise is that our ability, or lack of it, to deal with such sadness is actually something laid down many years before.

How we deal with saying our goodbyes and whether we can draw a line under an experience and walk away or bog ourselves down in misery, is a skill we learn at our parents' or carers' knees. But this is not just a question of what you yourself have undergone in your life. It also has a lot to do with the messages that your family passes on to you about facing up to leaving and letting go and to sadness. All families teach those within them the hard and sad rules of loss; but some families teach you how to deal with it and some, how not to.

Sandra, for instance, is an example of someone who learned lessons that undermined her ability to cope with bad things happening to her. Sandra came from a family that seemed to be happy and together. She had a younger brother with whom she got on well and her parents never seemed to have any arguments or even minor disagreements. Sandra excelled at school. She never failed an exam and got top grades in all her final tests. As far as friends were concerned, Sandra seemed to have experienced the same golden touch. Sandra was one of those people who always seemed to have a wide circle of friends, and never seriously argued with any of them. She was never dumped by any of her boyfriends nor did she dump them. All her relationships just 'sort of tailed off' and she remained friends with most of her past boyfriends. She went to university, got a First Class degree and married the young man she had been seeing for most of her time at college. Sandra sailed through life with very few problems or hold-ups, until she was 27. Then, she encountered what felt like her first setback in life. Sandra applied for her dream job and was turned down. At which point, to the total surprise of all her family, she tried to kill herself.

In fact, Sandra's reaction to what she and everyone else felt was the first and only time she had ever faced a failure would have been less of a surprise if she had had the opportunity to examine herself, her family and her background more carefully. In the aftermath of her suicide attempt, Sandra saw a counsellor. On one level, you could say that Sandra never learned to cope with an ending because she had been protected from ever having to acquire that skill. Since her life had been so charmed, she simply hadn't come face to face with failure and didn't know what to do. But not being given a chance to learn about sadness and loss is often an indication that there is more going on under the surface than simply being lucky. What emerged in Sandra's story was that there was a pattern in her family of avoiding looking at problems, and at endings. Sandra said that her parents never fought or argued. What she realised actually happened was that fights and arguments happened behind the scenes, hidden and denied. When tempers were lost, silence and disapproval made it clear that such behaviour was not to be tolerated. Any anger that anyone in her family felt or expressed was swiftly smoothed away. Disagreements – just like her relationships – 'tailed off' without a proper and conclusive ending. When something nasty happened, it was avoided and wasn't talked about. Sandra remembered that at the age of ten her mother had an argument with her closest friend. There were no recriminations or raised voices but somehow this woman was never spoken of, spoken to or seen again. It was as if she had been 'edited out' of her mother's and the family's life. When she was eleven, the family cat, who had been a part of the family for as long as Sandra could remember, died. It had been taken to the vet and simply didn't return. Nothing was said openly. Tears might have been shed, but in private and quietly. A new kitten appeared a week or so later and the old cat was never mentioned again. So all through her life Sandra had seen how negative motions were tidied away and ignored. She learned that both little and large endings were so frightening and the feelings they aroused feared to be so overwhelming that they simply weren't allowed to happen. Nothing ever ended in Sandra's family and in her life. Friendships, events, people 'tailed away' in an ending that wasn't an ending because everyone either pretended they hadn't existed in the first place or the leave-taking was so extended it faded away with no clear finish. What she had been trying to ignore just before she attempted suicide was the fact that her husband had been saying, at first quietly but later with greater force, that he had doubts about their relationship. He had been about to tell her he wanted a divorce when she took an overdose.

So, until she had the opportunity to consider it, Sandra would have said that she had such difficulty coming to terms with painful events because she'd never really faced any. Bill, on the other hand, was an example of someone who might have said they'd had plenty of losses in their life. One of his grandfathers died when he was a baby, both his grand-mothers died within six months of each other when he was seven, and his remaining grandfather died when he was ten. All of them had had regular contact with him, looking after him after school and during holidays. Bill's younger sister died in a car crash when he was thirteen and she was eleven. However, both Sandra and Bill shared one thing which is that in their families of origin unhappy feelings were swept under the carpet and unhappy events were dealt with by being ignored. Bill had not been taken to see any of his grand-parents during their final illnesses or his sister after her death. He was denied the opportunity to say a final farewell because he was not allowed to go to any of the funerals. Bill's parents did their best to protect him from their own grief and pain by being brave and not crying in front of him and by reassuring him that after death people went to heaven, a happier place. The message to a young person, of course, was that heaven was far more attractive than staying behind to be with him which put him thoroughly in his place.

DENYING THE UNPLEASANT

Many of us have moments when we prefer to disregard some-thing hurtful or unpleasant, and try to make it go away by ignoring it. Both Bill's and Sandra's families carried this to an extreme. Anything unpleasant, whether a situation, a person or an emotion, was covered up. In such families, anger and pain and other negative emotions are seen as so frightening and so dangerous that the fear is, once faced, they may be totally overwhelming or destructive. But plenty of us deal in similar ways to loss or endings, too. Without realising it, we are often scared that if we once acknowledge our anger or pain, it might sink us entirely. We may be scared that if we unleash rage it could be so powerful and destructive that the person we're angry at might never recover. Or that the hurt we feel may be so great it would paralyse and destroy us. So we may sit on it rather than let it out the bag. The result of this isn't that anger, pain or sadness vanishes. What happens is that it continues, under the surface. It's contained, but usually bursts out sometime, somewhere or somehow. Bill and Sandra adopted family patterns of running from and trying to ignore conflict and pain. Sandra kept hers at arm's length until some-thing so obvious happened that she couldn't ignore it, when she was turned down for the job she'd told everyone she wanted. At which point, she also had to face up to the fact that the one event she'd been trying to ignore was finally on the horizon – the bust-up of her relationship. Up until then, her coping mechanism had always been that of her family, to smile and pretend everything was fine and to turn away from arguments and messy emotions. Bill's way of coping with his fears was to keep them at arm's length and not to get too involved. He had affairs, frequently and regularly. He also had another way in which he dealt with the pain of endings, which we'll look at later.

COPING MECHANISMS

Acting in a particular way in order to deal with something that makes us unhappy is called a 'coping mechanism'. Children have a wonderful coping mechanism that they use among themselves to deal with anything unwanted. If one child says something to another that they don't want to hear, the second child will often stick their fingers in their ears and sing or shout loudly to drown out the unwanted words. If one tries to show the other something they don't want to see they will cover their eyes and turn away. Adults have more subtle coping mechanisms but these tend to be just slightly more sophisticated ways of covering eyes, sticking your fingers in your ears and going 'La, la la' at the top of your voice.

A common coping mechanism, then, is simply to avoid what is bothering us. Sandra's parents didn't argue because it was too frightening, too painful and she learned to do the same. There were no raised voices and no outward anger. What there was, however, was just as, if not more, destructive and effective. Veiled disapproval can be far more hurtful and long-lasting than an explosion of anger, and Sandra learned to fear her mother's silent rage. The problem, of course, with ignoring hurt and anger in the belief that if you pretend they're not there they will go away, is that nothing of the sort happens. Lack of communication and difficulties in a relationship are not improved by not talking about your feelings; on the contrary, the situation gets worse. But if you grow up in a family that believes 'least said, soonest mended' you may not learn the skills to start or engage in a discussion. You may only learn how to avoid.

Why may we turn away from the things we fear? It probably comes from a deep, ancestral memory that says if you lie still and pretend you're not there, the biggest trouble in your life will pass on by. This might have worked when the worst thing that could have happened to you was to be noticed by a sabre tooth tiger and turned into lunch. It's no longer applicable when your biggest fear may be you and your partner falling out of love with each other. We often operate on the superstition that if you don't put a name to something, it fades away. So, not saying there is a problem means the problem ceases to exist. Again, this doesn't work. And we also often go by the emotions we had as tiny babies. A small child has to learn momentous things while growing up – how to love and hate and how to deal with the seemingly impossible trick of realising you can both love and hate the same person or thing. A child loves the carer who shelters, cuddles and feeds it. But when anything the baby wants – a feed, a cuddle – is delayed, the child can be swept with terror and anger, feelings which can seem enormous and powerful.

Children really do believe they are the centre of the universe, and all-powerful. They can become horrified at the thought that, if their anger was truly unleashed, they might actually harm their parents or themselves. If you come from a family in which anger and any other uncomfortable feelings or the finality of loss are avoided or denied, this fear of the power of emotions and their destructive effect if allowed free rein, seems confirmed. You may find that the idea of facing feelings, of bringing anything to an end or a halt, or of accepting that something is over, virtually brings on panic attack. This makes facing up to endings so very hard.

If we're scared of endings, whether it's death or divorce, losing touch or turning way, we may find ourselves falling into a variety of coping mechanisms. One may be refusing to see any problems, or acknowledging that there are difficulties. One partner may insist the couple never argue and that everything in the garden is lovely. The other may try to raise concerns over a period of time and find their mate simply doesn't hear them. When, in desperation, the unhappy partner finally leaves, asks for a separation or otherwise makes their feelings felt in no uncertain manner, they may be astounded to hear the other swear, with apparent sincerity, that they had no idea the relationship was in trouble. Another common coping mechanism that occurs in unhappy relationships is for one partner to have an affair.

HAVING AN AFFAIR

One of the most common reasons given for the ending of a relationship is that one or other, or both, members of a couple have an affair. When an affair happens there is a range of explanations that we will usually give ourselves and other people. Men may claim that it meant nothing, was just sex and since it was offered on a plate they would have been crazy to have turned it down. Both men and women may argue that the affair happened because they fell in love with the other person and simply couldn't resist acting on this, in spite of the potential difficulties or hurt to other people. Frequently they, and indeed their partners, may argue that everything in the marriage was fine until this other person came along. The betrayed partner may paint the other man or woman as a seducer and blame them entirely, while the betrayer may claim that the new person, and new love, simply overwhelmed them. There is an alternative explanation which is that affairs are a coping mechanism to get over facing up to an ending. On the whole, affairs don't come out of the blue and don't happen in well-founded, happy relationships. By the time an affair begins, a relationship is usually already beginning to show cracks or come apart. It could be argued that for someone who doesn't want to face an ending, an affair provides a new beginning that can paper over and obscure the ending that they may otherwise have had to confront. Have an affair, and you can fix your mind on that and drown out any feelings which you may have about your other relationship finishing.

There are many coping strategies that can be used that allow us to hide the fact, from other people and from ourselves, that all is not well in our particular happy-ever-after. Carrying on an affair or a series of affairs may be one way of avoiding an ending, by ensuring that a new relationship starts before another can end. This may be a pattern of behaviour that started as a teenager when you first began dating. Early relationships can be intense even though they may be short-lived, and part of the learning experience in adolescence is to go through both falling in and out of love. The high and lows can be both exhilarating and painful but both extremes of early love are enormously valuable. In a sense, learning how you stop loving or being loved is the most important bit. How you cope with being left or leaving allows you to learn how to deal with disappointments and with endings. If, however, the pattern you evolve is one in which endings are fudged this may be not only an expression of how you have been taught how *not* to deal with endings, but also a way in which you may not learn how to do so. When Ali and Meera came to counselling it became clear that Ali had started an affair very soon after he and Meera began to experience problems in their marriage. When he looked back over his life Ali realised that he had never finished one relationship before going on to the next. In both his previous marriage and all his previous relationships Ali had met his new partner before ending the relationship with his previous one. In effect, he had never experienced an ending – he had always had a new one in place to go to for reassurance and solace before leaving the one before.

OBSCURING ENDINGS

But there are other ways of obscuring endings and their pain. The most common is to string out the experience, refusing to finish and make a clean break. Teenagers do this all the time. They may 'two time' by starting to see someone new, blow hot and cold in a relationship, or just avoid a boy or girlfriend but never actually tell them 'It's over'. Often what the avoider may be doing is trying to shift the responsibility for ending it onto the other person. Sally and Jake came to counselling when it had become clear to Jake that Sally was unhappy with their marriage. She no longer shared a bed with him, had made her own friends and a social life and frequently talked of leaving and of the fact that she no longer loved him. She constantly delayed actually moving out and came up with a range of excuses for delaying the move. When people string out the experience of making an ending the excuse is often that they are letting the other person down gently. Sally couldn't bring herself to say their marriage was over, cleanly and clearly. They would argue and she would say she was leaving but when he begged her to give it another chance, she would do so. She'd avoid him for days at a time but then cook him dinner and be nice. To her friends, she argued that she didn't want to hurt him and that it was kinder to pull away gradually. The reality in a situation like this however is that the only feelings that were being cushioned were Sally's. She couldn't face up to the guilt of causing Jake pain. It was Sally who was being let down gently, not Jake. His feelings were in a constant turmoil, alternately feeling hope and hurt while Sally was practising getting away from him but never actually doing it. Sally did not want to be the one to make the final decision and so be responsible for breaking up the marriage. Without realising it, all her efforts were concentrated on goading Jake into throwing up his hands and walking away so that she didn't have to feel that the responsibility had been hers. In the end, just as she had secretly hoped, Jake spared Sally the effort of making an ending, by doing it himself.

TRIAL SEPARATIONS

Another common way that some people fudge an ending is to make use of a trial separation. One of the partners may move out, going to live with friends, parents or other relatives or renting a home, saying they or the couple needs time to get sorted out. But trial separations often end in a permanent split: for some people, it's a way to begin to make a separation. The evidence is that, whatever couples say at the time, a trial separation is the beginning of the end. A study carried out some years ago by the University of Newcastle-Upon-Tyne with Relate appears to bear this out: only a quarter of the couples in the study who came for help after embarking on a trial separation were still together six months after the counselling ended.

A trial separation is often no more than a bridging exercise to making the final emotional leap into divorce proceedings. There are several reason for this. One is that once you've separated, it's far more difficult to come back together. Separation, even if it is supposedly temporary, makes all the problems in the relationship public. Friends and relatives tend to take sides. Everybody gets upset and if one partner spends the trial separation talking about what is wrong with the marriage, friends are likely to react with astonishment or even hostility if the couple eventually decide to get back together. When feelings are running high and there are rows and arguments in a relationship, there may well be justification for partners taking 'time out' from each other to cool down and reflect. But this is often best done in the relationship, not out of it. There is also a particular difficulty in trial separations when children are involved. Children tend to hope, when their parents separate, that they will get back together. A trial separation can be confusing and distressing if a parent does not return home after all. Once, couples may have opted for a trial separation because of the stigma of divorce. Rather than come out directly with the terrible, shaming news that the relationship was over, they slid into it to save face and delay the final admission. Now, trial separations may be more about a sense of failure, of not wanting to admit to each other or themselves that the relationship is completely finished. It may seem like the mature and sensible thing to do, seeking an adult solution to your problems. What you may actually be doing is embarking on the long goodbye, but not wishing to face up to that fact.

Some people avoid endings by never actually making them. There are couples who live in a 'shell' marriage – a marriage or relationship in which there is very little love or interaction. To the outside eye it all seems busy, happy and together. These may be couples who work together or who pursue intense and time-consuming pastimes together or apart. They may follow a sport, be constantly renovating their home, go to the pub or weekend car-boot sales together, or indeed raise a large family. They may be going through the motions but, deep down, the emotional link between them has ended a long time ago. All the activity both prevents and relieves them from ever having to look at their own relationship or from having to make a physical ending.

Another avoidance technique is for one or both members of a couple to focus on a continuing argument after the relationship breaks up. There is frequently conflict about children – access, upbringing – or about money. Bitter fights may go on for months or years, with both parties being able to give convincing explanations as to why they are doing what they are doing, feeling what they are feeling. The truth may be that what is really going on is that either or both are simply using whatever it is to keep the link and to try and gain or keep control. Money, particularly, is used to maintain one partner's control over the other. Penny, for instance, divorced her husband when he left her for another woman. He paid her an allowance for their daughter but also for herself, since Penny had left college to marry him and start their family and had never worked. After three years she decided she wanted to go back to college and get a qualification but her husband threatened to cut off her money if she did. She agonised for months over how she could manage if she defied him before suddenly realising that she was dancing to his tune as much as she had when they were – unhappily – married. Much as he might deny it, as long as she took his money for herself, not just for her daughter, he was still her protector and husband, even though he was married to someone else. Every time they argued about it, it was as if they were still married. And however much he had said and demonstrated he preferred being with another woman, what his actions showed was that he still wanted her at his beck and call. So she told him that what he thought or felt about her choice was none of his damn business. He would continue to provide for his daughter, or she'd take him to court, but she would make her own arrangements to finance her education. Her life was her own and, since their divorce, nothing to do with him. Once she realised his use of money was a way of remaining in her life, and keeping her in his, and that she'd fallen in the trap of accepting that, she could free herself of both her fears and her dependence.

THE SIGNS ARE THERE

When relationships end, we often say that it was a total surprise – that we never saw it coming. In fact, the signs are often there for all to see, some time before a partnership really hits the rocks. Some relationships seem to come apart suddenly and unexpectedly. Generally, they do so gradually, following what could be seen as an almost set pattern. The ending can frequently be predicted, if we were willing to acknowledge that such a thing was a possibility. The problem often is that, in trying to avoid an ending, we make it certain. After all, if you could see the rocks and admit that they are there, you could steer away from them.

A common pattern in relationship break down is this. When one or both people in a couple starts to be dissatisfied, they try to put up with it. Perhaps they begin to recognise that they have different priorities in the relationship – one wants children, the other doesn't, one has work ambitions, the other doesn't. Or maybe it's simply a case of no longer finding the other as attractive as they once did. Or maybe, after a few years together, they each have interests they don't share. Whatever, neither talks about their feelings but soldiers on as if nothing was wrong. After a time, mild dissatisfaction changes to irritation. At this point, the unhappy partner may drop a few hints that all is not well. It may lead to minor rows – nothing serious. They may also begin to be a bit moody and even to suffer regular, if unimportant, illness – headaches, stomach aches, back aches. Consciously or not, they may be wanting to draw attention to the 'sickness' in the relationship by asking their partner to notice how poorly they feel. If this doesn't trigger a face-to-face about the state of the relationship, the uneasy partner may shift into high gear and start going outside the relationship for fulfilment. This could be in the shape of a new job, new friends, new hobbies – or an intensi- fication of one or all. Someone who has merely dabbled in playing darts may suddenly join a team and be away reg- ularly, competing in matches. They may throw themselves into voluntary work, join an evening class or encourage other members of the family to do something that they can help or spectate at. Or, they may get into abusing alcohol or other drugs as a way of seeking distraction. Whatever, they may suddenly be busy and involved, often with matters that seem demanding and unarguable. After all, who can complain at a partner for doing charity work or taking children to out-of-school activities?

At this point, however, either or both partners may become aware that they are drifting away and that all this activity is coming between them and only widening a gap. One or both of them may make an effort to pull together, to get both of them sharing their lives and pastimes again. If this doesn't work, the moodiness and complaints will return, redoubled. At this point in the slide towards a break-up, not only will the unhappy partner turn away and invest heavily in time and effort spent doing their own thing; when they are at home, they will dig and bitch at their partner so rows and disagreements will be frequent and open.

This is the point at which an outsider is often drawn in. The unhappy partner will often now go looking for someone sympathetic, to offload their misery. They'll be needing and seeking someone to listen and someone who might help. It might be a friend or someone in the family, it may be a health care professional such as the family doctor, practice nurse or health visitor. It may be a relationship counsellor or a religious advisor, or a lawyer. Often, however, it is someone they meet at this point, to whom they transfer their romantic and sexual feelings. This person becomes more than a friend and is thus often blamed for the break-up, as if, had they not appeared, the relationship would never have broken down. In fact, the new relationship develops because the unhappy partner is ready, willing and able to let someone else into their life. And what began as a friendship may soon develop into something closer and more intimate than the relationship with the main partner. This may involve a romantic or sexual affair.

Once this has happened, the unhappy person may realise their relationship with the first partner is effectively over. They may still be living together, but as far as feelings are concerned, it has ceased to be a partnership. The unhappy person may then go through a stage of mourning the loss of that relationship, and putting it behind them. Eventually, they come to terms with the ending of the relationship. After this, they may end the relationship and leave. But if endings are a problem, the unhappy partner may stay where they are. The marriage or permanent partnership may remain, but the affair or a series of affairs may continue, and the relationship may stay together in name only.

CAN YOU FACE UP TO ENDING

For Bill and his partner Trish, the crunch point in their relationship came when Trish decided she'd had enough of his affairs. She insisted on going to counselling five years into their marriage. She had found out that he was seeing someone from work some six months previously and in spite of promising that it was over he was still in touch with this woman. To her knowledge this was the third relationship since they had been married but she suspected there had been more.

One feature that emerged pretty quickly in counselling was that Bill seemed unable to arrive on time. He would cancel at the last moment because he was running late and would regularly be five, ten or fifteen minutes late with what he felt to be perfectly valid reasons. He was most resistant to looking at his lateness and the counsellor had to be quite firm in doing so. Neither Bill nor Trish seemed to feel that his lateness had any bearing on what was going on in the marriage and were quite surprised when the counsellor said he wanted to discuss it because he felt that it did.

On this particular occasion Bill had been ten minutes late saying he had been held up at work in a discussion with a colleague. 'Ah' said the counsellor 'your colleague locked the door and refused to let you leave?' Bill laughed and said 'Of course he didn't.' 'Oh', said the counsellor, 'He took your car keys?' 'Well, no,' said Bill. 'I understand,' said the counsellor. 'You would have been sacked if you had left before you finished the work.' 'Well, no,' said Bill. 'So explain to me,' asked the counsellor, 'exactly how this person prevented you from leaving if they neither physically made it impossible for you to go nor threatened you with dismissal if you did.' What Bill finally had to face was that it wasn't the other person's insistence or actions that made him late, it was his own choice. One reason he may have made that choice was because he hadn't wanted to face up to the issues that were being discussed in their counselling sessions. But his inability to draw a line under a meeting, to finish up a talk, however trivial, and to end any one-to-one was part of the picture of their problem. Bill simply couldn't end any relationship or conversation. He used avoidance throughout their relationship to get round looking at the painful and unhappy feelings they had and Trish fell into the pattern, too. The affairs were just another way of bypassing what was going on between them.

Can You Deal With Endings?

You might like to consider whether you have difficulties in facing endings, by looking at issues other than your relationship. Ask yourself these questions:

* How do you end telephone conversations? Abruptly with a sudden goodbye? By spinning them out with repetition of what you've said, extra questions and remarks and gossip? Leaving both of you feeling the conversation has ended with nothing left unsaid but without going on too long?

- If you bump into a friend in the street and you are in a hurry, do you still tend to get caught up in a conversation you can't afford and keep trying unsuccessfully to break free? Cut them short and leave them feeling blocked? Say 'Hi, lovely to see you but must dash. I'll catch up with you later'.

- Do you enjoy books or films with sad endings or do you avoid them?

- When you visit a friend and know you've only got an hour do you spend the entire time on your feet watching the clock and leave early? Or are you still there after an hour and a half looking for an excuse to leave? Or do you relax for fifty minutes and spend ten minutes gracefully saying your goodbyes and leaving on time?

- Do you accept or hate funerals? Do you visit friends who are sick or avoid them?

- When you go to a party, are you always the first to leave, or the last, or does it vary?

- Do you have lots of friends from your childhood, school or college, or none at all, or have a few people you still keep in touch with because they are special friends?

There are no hard and fast 'right' or 'wrong' answers to these questions. But if you look at what you and your partner have answered, you may be able to see a pattern emerging that tells you something about the way you handle endings.

We tend to feel nowadays that we have a right to happiness. There is nothing wrong with working towards making the best of yourself, your relationship and your life but if you feel that you have been cheated and resent the fact that everything you've always wanted and expected *hasn't* dropped onto your plate, you are going to be in for a disappointment. Bad things happen, and you had better get used to it. This means that relationships can end and do end. There is no doubt that many relationships that founder and die could indeed have been saved, but not just by weeping, wailing and complaining or by saying 'It's just not fair!' If you want to pull a relationship back from the brink you will have to work at it. And if you are faced with the sad truth that you are in one that can't be saved, the best option for everyone concerned may be to make the best ending possible. You are not going to be able to save yourself and other people from sadness. You are likely to have to experience a whole range of uncomfortable and unpleasant emotions, but facing up to them and going through them is likely to be infinitely less painful and ultimately less destructive than trying to avoid the issue. In the next section we shall look at finding out whether yours may be a relationship that can be mended, and what to do next.

Chapter Two

CAN YOU MEND IT?

So, you think your relationship is at an end, what now? Many of us, if or when we realise that love seems to have faded, to be replaced by anger, conflict or bitterness, may like to stop it right there. The temptation is to reach for whatever means comes to hand to prevent any more pain. A hurried ending is often seen as preferable to dragging it all up or dragging it all out, as if getting it over with, with as little involvement or as much speed as possible, will make us feel better. We may not know how to deal with the emotions of loss and pain, or we may prefer to let someone else do it for us. So often we call in the people who seem to offer such help, such as solicitors or friends and family. All of whom appear to offer to protect your interests. Sadly, this may mean you are hurried too fast along the road to separation. Friends and family may assume that this is what you need. They may love you, but often have their own axe to grind and so can find it difficult to stand back and give objective advice. Many solicitors see their job as practical. They may feel their role is more to deal with the nitty gritty of separation than to consider whether this is in fact the best option and what you really want to do. Fortunately, more and more solicitors are now trained in mediation. Any solicitor who is a member of the Solicitors Family Law Association may well ask you to talk it over with a counsellor or mediator before going ahead. But many unhappy and battling couples still find themselves being ushered or even forced down the road of confrontation, when

what they really needed or wanted was a chance to off-load.
Before you assume a relationship is over, look at it carefully.
Don't shy away from asking for help, either in considering
whether you are at the end of the line or in rescuing the
relationship.

WHO TO TALK TO

The last person you should talk to when a relationship is
going wrong is a solicitor; the last, not the first. Solicitors are
there to help when the relationship is over or when violence is
threatened, not when you are unhappy, angry, confused or
need to put the relationship under the microscope to decide
what is going wrong, and what you want to do about it. The
person you should see first is someone in a counselling role.
This may be a counsellor, your own doctor or a community
leader such as a cleric.

   Don't see counselling as a last-ditch option, or one to be
shunned or ashamed of. Above all, don't assume your partner
wouldn't go. Agony aunts, doctors and counsellors themselves
are very used to being told 'Well, of course, I would go for help
but my partner wouldn't'. This is said more often by women
than men, and while it is true that men are often less willing to
talk, either with their partners or a professional, about their
feelings, it is often a very handy cop-out – some of those who
claim this haven't even raised the issue with their partners.
The truth is that if you can lay the responsibility for not
making an effort to rescue your relationship at your partner's
door, you can feel blameless. When people say their partner
wouldn't go, they often mean *they* won't. So, the first step to a
resolution, of whatever sort, is to consider 'Can we mend or
should we end this relationship?' And since it won't mend
itself, you're going to have to do something. Doing nothing is

an action in itself. For that reason, you may find it helpful to consider to what extent you are putting your life on hold, and how to free up your mind and your actions to making the necessary changes.

PUTTING YOUR LIFE ON HOLD

When life is hard, we often react by shoving what is worrying us on the back burner and promising 'I'll think about/do that later!' The longer you do it, the worse it gets. What we need to do is focus.

- **Focusing**
  Consider those times in your life when you felt everything went right, whether it was in love or at work. When everything falls into place, and just flows, it's usually because you knew exactly what you wanted and focussed on it. Like a small child who spots the toy they want on the other side of the room and heads off in pursuit, you concentrated and zero-ed in. To focus, we need to be aware of what we want, to be thinking about the here and now and to be clear about our interests and desires. We get what we focus on, which means that to be effective, we have to know exactly what that is. You will have two interests and desires at the moment. One is easy to name: to stop hurting. The other you may need to define. It may be that you want to get your relationship back on the rails, it may be that you want to separate. Of course, it may be that *you* want to get your relationship back on the rails but your partner doesn't, they want to separate and you don't. Part of your dilemma may be in having to come to terms and focus on an outcome that you don't want but may have to accept.

- **Stop being diverted**
  What usually stops us achieving what we want and need is that we get diverted. You may be pulled in several different ways when considering what you want, what you think you want, and by other people's needs and demands. That's why it's so essential to be clear on what's really important to you.

- **Making time for yourself**
  It's also vital to be clear about your own importance. You have as much right as anyone else to be happy, to have free time, good friends, treats and luxuries – and to love and be loved.

- **Being realistic**
  Sometimes it's hard to make decisions and focus because we're overwhelmed. It's important to reduce the unnecessary demand for perfection that many of us have. You can't be the Perfect Parent or Partner, the Perfect Son or Daughter, the Perfect Anything. All anyone can ever be is 'Good Enough', and that means setting your sights far more realistically. You can't focus on the important things in life – which are to love and be loved, to care and be cared for – unless you can recognise that there are more important things in life than being able to finish every task that you and other people set you. Shirley Conran once said 'Life's too short to stuff a mushroom', How true.

- **Break it down**
  It's easy to get thoroughly overwhelmed by any task if you look at where you are and where you want to be, and feel you must move from the first to the second in one leap. Breaking tasks down into manageable pieces goes a long way to reducing the anxiety that makes us avoid them.

- **Managing anxiety**
  Where there are problems, there is anxiety. Our fears and the paralysis that makes us get stuck comes from a voice

inside that nags on about all the ways we can fail, do it wrong, be incompetent. Focusing lowers our anxiety and increases confidence before even beginning the task. You may find it particularly helpful to clear your mind by trying some relaxation techniques. Lowering your heart rate, muscle tension and respiration rate through these can make you feel more comfortable and makes focusing easier. Try this:

Arrange a time when you can be alone and undisturbed – as little as ten minutes can make a difference though 20 to 30 is even better. Lock the door, switch off your phone and turn off the TV. If you have some gentle, soothing music play it softly in the background. Lie or sit down comfortably; if you're sitting, make sure your head is supported against the back of the chair. Close your eyes and slowly count from one to ten. As you do, concentrate on each part of your body, starting at your feet, while you first tighten and then loosen every muscle. Flex your toes and feet and then relax them. Move up your body, tensing and then relaxing your ankles and calf muscles. Move on to your knees and thighs, then your backside, each time first making rigid and taut, and then completely relaxing each set of muscles. Suck in your stomach and then your chest muscles, then shrug and pull up your shoulders. Move your neck. Tighten your biceps and make a fist. Pull a face so that all your facial muscles first strain then relax. When you've gone over the whole body a bit at a time, tauten the lot and then relax again. Then, slowly count from ten back down to one as you completely let go, ease off and let all the stress and tension you might be feeling flow out of you. Imagine the tension as waves, streaming out of your fingers and toes and out the top of your head, leaving you relaxed and free from pressure.

GOING LEGAL

When relationships go wrong, many people think that the first person to consult is a lawyer. This may be because talking to the legal profession that deals with divorce is the only action you can think of as being relevant. What many people expect when they go to see a solicitor to talk about divorce is that they will also get help, advice and an opinion on what is going on. They expect to be able to off-load their doubts, worries and unhappiness and to receive some sort of support and some suggestions as to what to do. This may indeed happen, or the solicitor may suggest you first speak to someone who can help in this role. Sadly, what sometimes happens is that they find themselves on a fast track to separation. On the whole, when it comes to separation and divorce, lawyers see their job as helping you sort out the legal aspects. They may not be able to help you look at your relationship and consider it. Since their responsibility is to their client – the person who comes to them – the situation can frequently and quickly become confrontational. They are there to fight your corner, to win on your behalf, and the point about there being a winner is that there has to be a loser. When it comes to the traditional, old-style legal profession the mode is of aggression and confrontation.

Fortunately there is a new breed of divorce lawyer who sees it differently. Not only are they trained to help you settle things more reasonably, they are also likely to suggest that you try counselling and mediation before you move into looking at the separation option. However the truth is that when we reach for a lawyer's help in a relationship argument it is because we want someone else to bring about the ending for us. We want to be swept through the process of having our relationship ended with the lawyer and the law taking the responsibility for doing this on our behalf. A hurried ending is often seen as preferable to having the reasons for the break down and our emotions about it dragged up and picked over. We don't know how to deal with the loss and pain.

But even a sympathetic and mediating solicitor is often the wrong person to go to in the first instance when you think your relationship is coming to an end. Even if it is finished you need to finish it for yourself, to close and draw a line and leave no unfinished business between you and your partner, before you untie that knot in a court of law. Whether your relationship is one of marriage or of long-term living together, the two people who should get together and clear the decks should be you and your partner, not you and your partner's legal representatives.

There are plenty of people ready willing and able to help couples explore and understand their relationship difficulties. The tragedy in this country and at this time is that we still have so many myths that prevent us from asking for such help and so many barriers against our accessing and using it. Every counsellor will tell you that the majority of clients who come for help start off by saying something along the lines of 'Well, we must really be at rock bottom to have ended up here'. Counsellors often have to bite their lips to stop themselves screaming 'So why didn't you come *before* you hit rock bottom?' The sadness is that if you see asking for counselling help as a proof that you have failed and so leave asking for help for too long, you make 'failure' almost inevitable. The stigma against asking for professional help means that its poor outcome is a self-fulfilling prophecy. Some 50 per cent of people who go to Relate will find that their relationships do break up, but this is not the failure of counselling. By leaving counselling until so late, the pain and the anger in your relationship may be so great that it's hard for anyone to turn it around.

STIFF UPPER LIP

There is a real tradition in our society that the only acceptable way of handling problems is to be strong, silent and to deal with your own problems. It's mostly a macho thing – real men don't cry and they certainly don't wash their dirty linen in public. While it's true that men, far more than women, will resist seeking help by spilling out their feelings it's also worth acknowledging we can put in other people's mouths what we are thinking or feeling ourselves. 'I would but he wouldn't', may sometimes mean 'I won't and he's a convenient excuse'. The main cause in this society, however, is the strong British ethic against making a fuss, calling attention to yourself and indulging in that messy stuff, emotions.

You don't necessarily need a professional to help you examine your own relationships and come to terms with any difficulties you are having. You and your partner could, with a degree of honesty and application, do this on your own. But I have to say that when people violently, angrily or defensively shy away from the very idea of asking for professional help, it doesn't show confidence in their ability to do it for themselves. The justification may be that you don't want interference, that you don't want to bother with all that 'psychobabble' and that you are perfectly capable of sorting out your own relationship, thank you. If this is what you are saying, close your eyes for a moment and be honest with yourself about what you are thinking. If the reality is that you don't want to go to counselling because you would rather not face up to what a professional might help you uncover, because you would rather go on with the games, the evasions and the self-deceit, then you have every right to do so, but at least be honest about it.

A SCARY OPTION

Counselling is a scary option because even if you don't know exactly what happens when you undergo counselling most of us are aware that it has to involve talking about areas that upset us. When we are going through an emotional crisis it's very tempting to want someone, anyone, to wave the magic wand and make it go away. If you think back to when you were a child and you fell over and hurt yourself, what were you most likely to do? You would have run to an adult to make it better, but you might have been quite insistent about what it was you expected them to do. A small child with a cut or grazed knee is likely to scream and howl at any suggestion of the area being cleaned and disinfected because that will hurt. What the child wants is for you to 'magic it' better. If you really can't wave the magic wand, say the magic words and kiss the pain and the bleeding goodbye then they might ask you to slap a plaster over the top and wait for it to go away. But anything else – no thank you! We are exactly the same with emotional wounds and we tend to get exactly the result that a child would have if allowed to go for the easy option. A cut or wound that is simply covered over will become infected and cause far more pain in the long run. Parents do not let children be their own worst enemies in these situations. We bear their pain and weeping, struggle to remove their hands and insist on doing the painful duty of making them better.

Sadly, when it comes to dealing with adult wounds we don't have people looking out for us. Professionals may suggest that we don't ignore our problems, but can't insist. Which is a pity because, just as with physical wounds, if you cover up an emotional hurt it is likely to return to haunt you. Time may heal the intensity and pain but it doesn't stop our reactions to it. Most of all it doesn't stop us applying the coping strategies we develop to deal with such pain to other less appropriate situations. You may get over the loss of someone you love early in life by protecting yourself from being hurt again. One quite common way of doing this is to make sure in relationships that you are the one who leaves before someone else has the chance to leave you. This may appear to be a good protective technique – you are never going to feel the heartache of being abandoned if you always leave the relationship before you get too intimate or before the other person has a chance to reject you. Mind you, you are also never going to have the opportunity to love or be loved. You may think you have got over the pain of having been left as a child, and you are not going to experience the pain of being left as an adult. What, of course, you may overlook is that neither are you ever going to experience the joy and the security of having someone stay with you.

What counselling can do is help you go back and explore what might have happened to you in your past and how you may have taken it – not just at the time but how you may still be reacting in ways that affect you in the here and now. Although individual counselling is often a useful option, it's often best to look at difficulties that are affecting your relationship as a couple. Very, very rarely can anyone say that whatever is happening in a relationship is one person's problem and not the other's. If nothing else, looking at the fit between you at least allows you properly to understand exactly what is going on in the mind of the one who seems to be feeling or causing the most difficulties. On the whole though a problem in, and with, a relationship tends to be a couple problem, one that needs to be sorted out with both and by both.

TALKING TO A STRANGER

Many of us tend to feel that going to counselling is like baring our intimate secrets in public, speaking to strangers about something we'd rather keep private. The advantage of going to counselling, to talking to a stranger, is that in fact it's far less revealing and embarrassing than it might be talking to the people you know. A professional, whether it's a doctor, a psychiatrist or a counsellor, is bound by a code of confidentiality. They may need to discuss your case with their own colleagues but it would be for professional reasons, to allow them to help you, not to gossip. No-one would ever hear of your problems, or even that you had visited them, without your expressed consent. And once your visits to them were over, the fact that you had gone would not return to haunt you. As an agony aunt I've frequently heard from people who desperately regretted asking for help, advice or support from those around them. Some had colleagues who blabbed to others which made the atmosphere at work embarrassing and hard; some had friends who had told them how they would deal with the situation and then became hostile and angry when they'd not taken the advice; and some had family members who had taken sides and could not change when the situation resolved.

Gita had gone through a difficult period in her marriage and during that time had confided in her mother. Her husband had been unfaithful and Gita, while being broken hearted and angry, still wanted to make it right. They had gone to Relate and had some painful sessions talking it through. But the result, she had felt, had been worth it. She believed his remorse, and his love for her led both of them through to a new and better understanding. She wrote to me, however, not for help with their relationship but in dealing with the unpleasant legacy of talking to her relatives. In spite of the fact that she still loved and now trusted her husband again, her mother was unrelenting in her hostility to him. She couldn't forgive her son-in-law and lost no opportunity in letting him know how she felt. Gita was left desperately regretting ever having talked to her.

It is very difficult for people who know you to be objective in the advice they give you. Sometimes this is because people who care about you are drawn to the pain and anger you may be feeling and respond to it. They may come back by giving you suggestions that link in specifically with those over-whelming negative feelings. So you tell them that your partner has done the dirty on you and they advise you to leave or fight back. Perhaps even more significantly anyone who hasn't had training in dealing with emotional problems will find them-selves having their own buttons pressed by your situation. Talk about marital infidelity, about anger that verges on violence, about being rejected, and anyone who has had that happen to them will be speaking to their own experience, not yours. You are going to get advice that is on the lines of 'If I could have done it, this is what I would have done', rather than on the lines of 'on sober reflection this might do for you'. A professional carer is specifically trained to deal with this sort of human response. They know that to help you best they shouldn't just be reacting to the buttons you push. They will stand back from your emotions and give you what you need – which is not always what you want, and certainly not what they might want. They will be able to separate their own impulsive response from what you actually should be hearing.

Professional counsellors are also particularly effective because they are likely to be tougher on us than our friends might be. If a friend makes a suggestion or wants to pursue a particular line of questioning and comes up against a barrier from you they are likely to back off. A professional counsellor is more likely to challenge you, particularly because the very areas we balk at are often the very ones that yield the answers.

The reason counsellors so often ask you the clichéed ques-tions about your parents is that they need to build up a picture of why you are where you are now and why certain things strike certain emotional chords. When you go into counselling the aim is to explore what is happening at the moment and what might have happened in the past. The counsellor will initially ask questions to help all of you build up a picture of what you see as having happened in the relationship and what you can remember as having happened in your childhood. In the next stage you will try and understand how all this fits together and finally you would be asked to take action, to work towards changing the things you would like to change. Counsellors aren't in charge during this process – you are. It's always a question of having options and making choices. But that doesn't mean to say that it's a cosy chat. While the choice to stay or continue always remains yours, a counsellor's job in order to do the best for you is to push you. In counselling you need to confront your feelings and your impressions and the counsellor is there to guide you through this maze and urge you on.

FEELING HELPLESS

It's very easy to feel helpless and in the grip of either fate or other people when a relationship is going wrong. A lot of us feel that we, our opinions and our feelings, don't count. Perhaps we went through school being told we wouldn't amount to much and at home felt we didn't matter much. Perhaps we've had jobs in which we've felt unvalued and relationships in which we felt essentially unneeded. You can come to a point in which you think that life and everyone around you either pushes you around or passes straight over you. Being told that you can make a choice can then seem like a very bitter joke. You never had choices before, why should you begin to have them now? And even if your life hasn't been quite as extreme as this, it's still easy to assume that you are a passenger rather than a driver. So maybe you are never going to be the one to decide whether England wins the World Cup or if we are going to join the European Monetary Union. The fact is, however, you do have choices and power and control in your own life. Doing nothing – just letting the influences around you push you on – is in itself a sort of choice. You are choosing to let other people decide.

WHAT DO YOU WANT?

You might have a clear idea of what you want from counselling. Some couples go wanting help with every intention of listening to advice and trying to put it into action. Some go with the same idea in mind but often have 'split agendas' whereby even though they may be saying they are in accord they are actually flying off in different directions. Some people go because they want the relationship to be mended, some because they want it to be ended. Some seek counselling as a means of having their say, of having a witness to what they feel and think, of making absolutely sure that the other person hears what they are trying to say. Some use counselling to prolong an argument, rather than finding a solution. Others wish to 'Beat the counsellor' and to demonstrate to themselves, to their partner, to the professional and to the world in general exactly how resistant to help they and their problems may be. A phrase that often comes up in letters to agony aunts is that 'Counselling doesn't/didn't work'. Not so, counselling works. The question is whether the people who went to it did. Counselling requires work. You have to put your heart and soul into it. It's painful, it's likely to hurt, and it certainly takes an enormous amount of effort. But if you are prepared to do the work you will get a result. It may not be exactly the result you wanted or said you wanted, but it will make a difference and there will be changes. The problem of course is that we don't always know exactly what we want or what we need. Because counselling deals with deep emotional issues not only is it painful and scary but it also often uncovers the unexpected. There is an old saying – 'Be careful of what you wish for, because you might just get it'. The wish of your heart may not be what you thought it was.

THREE OPTIONS

Relationships can, however, be recovered from a surprisingly long way down the slope to disintegration. Couples who have warred for years can be surprised at how possible it is to pull a partnership together again. You really have to choose one of three options.

Option one

Option one is to do nothing. It is quite possible to continue as you are. In spite of all your bitterness or unhappiness, you may actually decide that any other option is more unpleasant or unacceptable.

Option two

This is a slight variation on doing nothing, which is to at least gain some insight into why the two of you run your relationship the way that you do. You may have chosen your particular style of interaction and however uncomfortable it may feel it may fulfil the needs that both of you have. Couples who complain about their relationships but never seem to make a break can sometimes realise that their arguments or disagreements are actually part of what makes their relationship work. Three examples of relationships that do so are sometimes referred to as 'Babes in the Wood', 'Cat and Dog' and 'Net and Sword'.

- *Babes in the Wood* Babes in the Wood couples are couples who stick together like conjoined twins, as a twosome. They are each other's best, if not only, friends and huddle together – them against the world. It's as if they see the outside world as bad and dangerous and their only possibility of safety and happiness is being with each other, even when they're not getting on. Babes in the Wood couples tend not to have many close friends and their social life revolves around each other. When it comes down to it they reject everyone else and fly towards each other.
- *Cat and Dog* Cat and Dog couples are the ones who bicker and fight, not just in private but in public too. It's as if they are the direct opposite of Babes in the Wood and see their partners as being the essence of all that is terrible. They would far rather be with other people who they see as exciting and acceptable. Cat and Dog couples have plenty of friends and a social life that revolves around being with other people. They reject each other and fly towards others and yet, just like Babes in the Wood, they are held together as if by a pact.
- *Net and Sword* Net and Sword couples are an unhappy combination of the other two examples. While in Babes in the Wood and Cat and Dog couples both partners have the same impulse – to lean together or apart – in Net and Sword one of the partners would like to shut away the outside world and spend all their time with, and all their effort on, their partner. The other, however, is just the opposite and flings up barriers and turns away, seeing everyone else as far more acceptable and much more fun to be with. Net and Sword couples are opposites – one is a loner who would prefer to have a quiet life, the other wants to be out with the crowd as often as possible. But in all these, and other cases, couples can find themselves dancing around each other, complaining bitterly but seeming to be unable to make a break.

If you can understand why your particular relationship – with its arguments, isolation or high activity – has formed and how it functions, you may very well choose to leave it as it is. Understanding what needs it fulfils may at least reduce the conflict you have. If you can see that you recognise yourselves as a 'Babes in the Wood' partnership you may stop blaming each other or worrying about not having a wide circle of friends. If you can see that being 'Cat and Dog' is why you fight so much you can at least accept that it is actually nothing personal and each of you value each other – you just need to fight. If you can see that you are 'Net and Sword' you can accept the way one of you attacks and the other absorbs.

Option three

This is one that many people would like and need. Couples often come to a crisis point because they have built a relationship on a pattern which was right for them during a particular period. 'Me Tarzan, you Jane' might have been very comfortable when one of you felt they needed to be looked after, and the other could deal with their own insecurities, and need to be needed, by playing the role of the one in charge. The problem comes when one of you changes. In fact, it can still be a problem when both of you change because any alteration in a relationship, even when both partners are pulling in the same direction, can be difficult to accept and manage. But the real head-on clashes occur when one of you is struggling to burst out of the bounds of the framework you've set and the other is struggling to keep it as it has always been. It's very easy, when you are trying to deal with what are actually large changes in your relationship, to get bogged down in the minutiae. At a time when you should be talking about how you are feeling about yourselves, and how you see your relationship working, you find yourself arguing about who puts the rubbish out, who does the washing-up and what sort of discipline you want to bring to your children. What

professionals and counsellors are so good at is bringing us back
to what we really need to be discussing. We are often frightened
to go to a counsellor because at the root of partnership change
are immense, powerful and seemingly overwhelming emotions.
We may feel enormous anger, tremendous fear and massive
guilt. We may want to express all these but be terrified that if
we did, it would be so destructive. We are frightened that bringing these feeling out into the open would destroy our partner,
our relationships, our families and ourselves.

The sad thing is that these feelings are far more destructive
if kept under wraps. They can indeed do everything you fear
if you sit on them. If you and your partner feel you are at the
end of your relationship and are thinking about finishing it,
the reason may well be that you have problems you are too
scared to confront. The tragedy is that you could be walking
away from a relationship that would work because deep down
you feel the sadness of parting is a better option than the dread
of facing up to the reasons for your troubles. Of course, they
may indeed do what you fear if you simply unleash them.
What counselling allows you to do is to bring them out in a
place and a time of safety with someone skilled at containing
and interpreting these feelings. Couples who go to counselling
often find they can say the unsayable and at the end of the
session walk away. They can leave behind something which if
it had been said at home would have hung over them, causing
misery and arguments. While in counselling, it can be packed
away and left behind until the next session.

UNRECOGNISED NEEDS

It can be extremely hard to move on from a relationship if it is
founded on needs we don't recognise. Kath, for instance, asked
for help after her husband had left her. What she felt she

needed was advice on making him love her and wanting to stay. What emerged was a picture of an extremely abusive relationship with a man who hit her regularly and who was constantly, consistently unfaithful. Kath was convinced that she was missing something, that if she could just be nicer, sexier, better, he'd begin to be the person she thought he was when she fell in love with him and would love her and protect her. Kath was most resistant to the idea of looking at her childhood for ways to understand her present situation. Eventually she started talking about her father. He has been a wonderful Dad, she said, and her childhood had been very happy. Of course, her father wasn't always there. Her mother was a difficult woman, said Kath, who drove him away with her questions and her nagging which was why he had spent so much time with other women. Gradually a picture grew up of a far from happy childhood. Kath's father often beat her mother and was regularly unfaithful. But because he was her father and the first and main man in her life, Kath was desperate for his recognition and his love. He constantly evaded taking responsibility for his own actions, blaming his behaviour on his wife. And Kath, because all small children see themselves as the centre of the universe and blame themselves for anything that goes wrong, believed him. As is common in such situations, Kath was convinced that she could change things, that if she had been nicer, sweeter, better, her father would have been the father she needed and wanted and would have loved her and stayed with them. And since she needed to forgive him, as well as blaming herself she accepted his word that it was her mother's fault, and thus that women are to blame when relationships go wrong. All the relationships she had had in her life, up to and including her husband, were with men similar to her father – men who were abusive and who would not take responsibility for their own actions; men who fled commitment, who hit out when they were angry or felt guilty and who would not stay faithful.

Kath set herself an impossible task. She looked for men like her father in the hope that she could rewrite the script, that this time she would be able to be better so that they would love her. The task was impossible for two reasons. One was that she chose men who found it impossible to act in the way that she needed. Perhaps these men could, if they sought insight and understanding into why they behaved as they did, and changed themselves. But nothing Kath was going to do would change them. Indeed, her behaviour acted only as a spur. By continually being the victim she only reinforced their position as abusers. But the second reason why she was in a no-win situation was that the person she wanted to change was not the one with whom she was living. Even if her husband had undergone a transformation and turned himself into the caring, sharing man – the perfect husband and father – the likelihood is that Kath would still have felt that something was missing. In such abusive relationships, when the abuser does see the error of his ways, it's not unknown or unusual for the victim to up sticks and leave saying 'You've suddenly become boring'. The person Kath really wanted to be different was her father. If her husband had become loving and caring he still wouldn't have repaired the damage of the past. It was her father that Kath wanted to have been different in the past and rewriting the script in the present wasn't going to do that for her.

LOVE IS NO ACCIDENT

Kath's example might be at the extreme end of how our past leads us into destructive relationships in an attempt to rewrite what happened to us in our childhood. But when we look for a partner we are all, in one way or other, acting on needs set up in our childhood. Who you fall in love with is not the result of accident nor is it simply because that blue-eyed charmer or dark-haired sexpot is so attractive that anyone would fall in love with them. It's all a question of that blueprint. Kath was drawn to people who were careless of other people's feelings, who were violent and emotionally as well as physically absent, because that was what her father was like. You may find yourself falling for people with a ready smile, people good with their hands, people with a lot of suppressed anger or people with a need to be needed because that's what you have learned are the necessary constituents for the other person in your relationship. We build up our blueprint from all sorts of bits and bobs, experiences and feelings that gather around us as we grow up. Elements become necessary either because they remind us of the things that made us feel happy and secure in our families of origin. Or they are there because they are parts of a fantasy that we built up of the things that would have made us feel so much better.

FITTING THE JIGSAW

The person you fall in love with matches that blueprint. They fit in, they become the bits of the jigsaw that complete the puzzle. Sometimes what completes your puzzle may be things that seem to match you and are the same as you. So you will get two adventurers who are prepared to sell up and hike around the world together, two people who have a total lack of concern for worldly goods, or two people who haunt car boot sales and fill their house with collectibles. But more often what completes your picture is something that is complementary. The bold and adventurous person falls for someone quiet who likes to stay in the background. The extremely sociable falls for the stay-at-home. The optimist goes for the pessimist. 'Opposites attract' is accurate and for a good reason. Together you form a whole. If there's something that rather alarms or scares you that doesn't fit in with your own personality you'll choose a partner who will do it for you. If your way of dealing with the world at large is to sit quietly in the corner and observe it, you may find yourself being attracted to the person who dances on tables and talks to everyone. As one half of your couple they can express your sociability while you can express their calmness. Each of you will be balanced by the other, each of you will be let off doing whatever it is the other one does for you.

This is also why we often seek out partners who deal with emotions in a different way to ours. Haroon, for instance, came from a family in which anger was taboo. He never saw his parents have an argument and he learned very early that he was only acceptable to them and indeed loveable to them when he was 'nice'. No-one ever lost their temper in Haroon's family because to do so was absolutely unacceptable. Haroon was a pleasant, smiling and cheerful fellow who was often during his teenage years blinded by tension headaches. He fell passionately in love with Carla and the only thing he found extremely uncomfortable about her was the fact that she had a hair-trigger temper. Both of them found having disagreements acutely uncomfortable. Carla's way of dealing with a conflict was to scream, shout, slam doors and throw things. Haroon's way was to state his case calmly and then sulk, tight-lipped, for three days. Both hated the way the other reacted and tried their best to make the other feel bad and change. It was a friend who pointed out that perhaps it was no co-incidence that apart from this each felt the other was their soul mate. Perhaps, said the friend, this was actually part of it. Haroon's background made him feel acutely embarrassed at such an overwhelming, over-spilling of emotion. Carla's made her unused to restraint. Carla expressed Haroon's need for abandonment, Haroon expressed her need for a bit of control. Far from it being a problem in their relationship it was really the sand in the oyster. That is, the little bit of grit that becomes a pearl. Once they could accept it and see it as part of the jigsaw, then they could forgive and see it as the other's way of handling conflict. They learned to make a bit of a joke about it and gradually Carla became a bit less over-the-top and Haroon a little bit more so.

Haroon and Carla are an example of the way that marital fit may work for a couple. The way we may be drawn to another person to complete that jigsaw – another person who fulfils a lot of the 'person specification' we have in the blueprint we have built up in our childhood – can lead us however into relationships that carry the seed of their own destruction. The blueprint can lead you to falling for an abusive partner in an effort to rewrite an unhappy childhood script. But it can also lead you to find a partner who in appearing to satisfy that need gives you a relationship with a very short time limit. Jennifer, for instance, never knew her father. He and her mother parted before she was born and her mother never remarried. Jennifer's first serious boyfriend was ten years older than her and she eventually married someone twenty-five years her senior. 'May/December marriages' may often work when the age of the partners is not the most important thing in their relationship but is incidental. Whether Jennifer liked to recognise it or not, her husband's age was the most important thing about him. They were very happy for several years and then the marriage ran into trouble. They began to argue over seemingly trivial matters and the arguments tended to follow a similar pattern. Jennifer would snap at her husband, he would answer mildly and reasonably and she would work herself up into an uncontrollable rage. After several sessions with a counsellor he offered the interpretation that Jennifer had initially been happy to have found her perfect father. Her husband was mature in years and also in attitude and tended to be calm, rational and understanding. But Jennifer had now fulfilled her fantasy of having an older man offer her security and protection. She had run through it and no longer needed it and now wanted to grow up and leave home. In essence she was playing out being a teenager and rebelling against her kind daddy. The arguments were preparation for what all teenagers should do, which is leave home.

REWRITING THE SCRIPT

In any relationship in which either one or both of the partners is attempting to rewrite the past, particularly putting a new ending on past experience, the relationship may implode when circumstances or emotional needs change. You may have found yourself a partner who will act like a parent to you or indeed act like a child to your parent. You may find someone who needs to be cared for to your carer, petulant child to your serious adult. You may find someone that wants to lie back and let you get on with it or is happy to take over totally and allow you to coast. The relationship will continue on an even keel as long as both of you are perfectly happy with the roles you are playing. And if either of you wishes to change, there will again be no difficulties if the other is prepared to alter too. What frequently happens, of course, is that when the goal-posts are moved one person is not only caught off balance and unprepared but finds themselves unsatisfied with the new rules. You may find the relationship not only running into trouble but drawing to an end. And it may not only be an end that neither expected, but that neither of you is comfortable in handling. This will be not only because endings are sad and difficult but that the nature of it leaves you confused. You don't know why what seemed to be the perfect relationship has suddenly hit the rocks. What has caught you on the hop is that just as the underlying need you had had for each other was based on needs you hadn't fully recognised, so too its ending is out of your grasp.

We often shy away from examining a relationship that's not giving us happiness and doing anything about it for two reasons. One is that the pain of looking at what has gone wrong, and why, seems too much to bear. But the other is that the act of looking means taking action. While we turn our backs we can go on as we are. Scratch the surface and we are going to have to make a decision one way or another and that decision may have to be-to finish. The saddest aspect of all this is that ignoring what is happening in an ailing relationship is more likely to lead to its death than looking at it.

What If It Had Changed?

Ask yourself, if you woke up tomorrow and whatever was making you unhappy had stopped, what might have changed? This game has two sides to it. One is that, if you are honest with yourself, it can help you work out if your relationship is ending or might respond to work. For instance, if your answer was 'We wouldn't be arguing', you may want the relationship to be better. But if your truthful response is 'We wouldn't be together' it could indicate you would rather the relationship would end. The other aspect is that your answers may give you a clue as to what aspect of your relationship you may need to focus on. Carla's answers were 'I wouldn't feel angry, he wouldn't be sulking, he'd love me and understand me'. When she looked at what she said, she began to realise that her own actions created many of the misunderstandings with Haroon. It was the issue of anger and how it was expressed that was the trouble in their relationship, and both their fears that each might stop loving the other. While her over-the-top anger was her way of expressing her feelings, and may indeed be part of her appeal to the quieter Haroon, it proved difficult for him to cope with. When she realised she had to confront her own way of arguing as much as he had to deal with his, both of them reached a compromise.

Of course, the professionals you may need to consult about difficulties in your relationship may not necessarily, or only, be those that deal with your emotional wellbeing. Nico and his wife Maria came to the brink with their relationship when he became impotent. Nico started having difficulty first in keeping, and then in getting, an erection and so started making excuses and avoiding having sex. He also avoided touching, kissing or showing any affection towards Maria because he felt so guilty and inadequate about having no response to touching her. Maria in turn felt rejected and then angry and their formally happy marriage went downhill rapidly. After a year of anger and bitterness Nico happened to be called in for a check-up by his doctor at work. A simple ten-second test revealed that he was suffering from diabetes, a condition that often leads to erectile difficulties. Nico and Maria had found that a relationship that had few problems beyond the fact that they didn't communicate as much as they should, had been severely tested because of a physical problem. Both had put an emotional interpretation onto what was happening, added two and two and come up with six. Nico felt inadequate and guilty, Maria felt rejected and unvalued, when what was actually going on was a physical reaction to a medical condition, not a lack of love or manliness.

WE'RE NOT MIND READERS

However long you may have lived with your partner you can't read each others minds. We frequently misinterpret what someone does or says because we take it personally. One person comes home from a day in which everything has gone wrong, and sulks and snaps. The other concludes that they are being blamed, that they are being rejected and snarls back. Before you know it you are in the middle of a full-scale row, the basis of which is that each partner felt got at and unloved by the other because of what they said or did. In reality what they said and did may have had everything to do with other things in their life and little to do with the person they love. Failure in desire and in sexual ability or enjoyment may well be to do with what is going on in the relationship. Sex is often the first thing that goes by the board when our love is waning. We may not want to make love when we are angry with our partner or feel that they haven't heard us. Withholding sex is a way of withholding love and is thus a way of making a point. The failure in sexual desire is also often a result of personal depression and lack of self-esteem. Or, it may be caused by physical illness or by treatment. A wide range of medication will affect our ability to feel aroused and our ability to either erect or lubricate, and any mood-changing medication that softens out the lows of depression will equally affect the highs of love and affection. While it cannot be stressed too highly that you shouldn't reach for physical explanation in order to excuse or to shy away from emotional involvement, it is worth considering what else is going on in your life before assuming that the problems you are experiencing in your relationship mean that your love is in trouble.

OTHER ASPECTS

As already said, relationship problems may have more to do with other aspects of your life than the relationship itself. You may be playing out arguments, miseries or grudges that really should be laid at the feet of other people, not your partner. When a relationship hits a problem it's always worth asking yourself when the difficulties started and what

changed at that time. Was there a change or a crisis in the
family that might have affected your view of your life or your
relationship? You can't, for instance, expect your life or your
love to be the same if someone in your family has just
died. If it's a grandparent or a parent your whole world view
will have been altered. You may suddenly see yourself as a
totally different person. Where yesterday you were a child or
grandchild, today you may feel a full adult and even head of
your family. This is going to affect the dynamics of your relationship. After all, if it's based on both of you seeing you as
a person who needs looking after, being propelled into full
adulthood can change that uncomfortably. If it's a brother or
sister, or even a brother- or sister-in-law, or a close friend,
that will affect your feelings of mortality and security.
Suddenly you may realise that you are at the age where you
could die too, and you may decide life is too short to stay in
a situation that gives you no joy. And if it's a child of your
own or someone close to you that too may lead you to suffer
feelings of guilt, anger or pain that are likely to have a dramatic effect on your relationship. Death and loss are perhaps
the most dramatic and obvious influences but there are many
others that can bring to bear on your relationship. Changes in
employment, moving house, the arrival of children and the
various milestones in their lives, can all bring pressure on
how you feel about yourself and yourselves. And all can
put your relationship under the microscope. Before assuming
that you've run into troubles you can't deal with, that
your arguments or disagreements mean you will have to
part, take the trouble to look at whether you can mend it.
There are many reasons why such reflection before deciding
to break up is important. One is that both the relationship
and the difficulties you have with this particular person
may not be unique. Each of you brings half of what makes a

relationship to the table; which means you also bring half of what is breaking you apart. Throw up your hands and walk on to the next one and you may find that you bring to that partnership exactly the same elements that led to your leaving this one. Unless you can look at why it's ending, you are likely to repeat the process in the next relationship, too.

Talking together

If you and your partner feel you are at the end of the line and about to split up, it's possible that you or they are convinced the other can't or won't listen or co-operate. We often sabotage our own attempts to improve communication as a couple by being convinced it's futile. What stops a lot of us in this situation is the fear of being made vulnerable, of being the one to show our emotions and need. We can also delay trying to change a situation that we really do want to be different because, until we have tried, there is always hope. Our worry may be that if we try and it doesn't work out, we are then really stuck. What we can miss in this is that our partner may have exactly the same fears and exactly the same wish to alter things and make them better. The bottom line is that you will never know if you haven't tried asking them – and it is always worth asking. Use these strategies to talk to your partner about what it is you might think has changed and might like to be different. Aim to open the lines of communication again, if for no other reason than to be able to discuss a near-at-hand break-up. Learning to communicate better may help you to turn back from the brink of an ending. If an ending is inevitable, at least it can help you to deal with your feelings and part with dignity. If you have children, it can certainly be vital in helping you to *parent* together even if you are no longer going to *be* together.

Taking Turns

This is a game for you and your partner to learn how to
hear when the other wants to talk to you, and talk in turn
so the other will hear you. Begin by sitting, facing each
other, and agree that you will take it in turns to be the
speaker and the listener. Negotiate a period of time to be
used – say two minutes to start with. During this period
the speaker should talk about anything they want or feel
they need to say. The most important rule is that it should-
n't be criticising or blaming, but offering an explanation of
how they feel about something important to them. And
they must talk for the full two minutes. As they talk, the
listener's job is to hear and encourage them to go on – but
without themselves saying a single word. This means that
the listener must not make comments, ask questions or
interrupt in any way. Instead, they should help the speaker along with gestures and nods and the sort of sounds of
attention that give the speaker the message of 'Go on. Yes,
I'm listening to you and hearing you'.

Have more than one go at this. You will get the best
results by trying it quite a few times. After your first
attempt, both of you should talk over what it was like.
How did it feel, for example, having to just listen and not
be able to ask questions or interrupt? What was it like to
be listened to, uninterrupted? Both will probably have
been new experiences because most of us are not used to
talking or listening in this way. Our more usual practice is
to chip in, finish sentences for the other person, or ask
questions, and none of this exactly helps good communication. When the subject is personal, especially over
ground we've argued about, we try to put our own point of
view. The reasons we act this way are to do with stopping
the other person saying things we don't want to listen to,

or to our wanting to take control of the situation. Even on the occasions when we do genuinely want to listen we can find it hard to let the other person have a true opportunity to voice their feelings clearly, simply because we're not used to just listening without interrupting in some way. We also often listen in a distracted, hostile way, showing by inattention that we don't like what we're hearing.

When you do stand back, give the other person a clear run and make it clear you are listening properly to what they are saying; it can both reassure and empower them. This is because knowing they are being heard gives the speaker a chance to hear themselves, too. They don't have to spend time and energy trying to catch and hold your attention or dragging you back onto the subject of what they wanted to talk to you about in the first place. Trying 'active listening' techniques may seem a bit odd and awkward on first attempts but you should soon get used to them and be somewhat astounded at just how useful and effective they are as tools for good communication.

Once you've tried the 'active listening' approach to communicating, move on a stage further to trying the skills of 'reflective listening'.

Reflective Listening

As in Taking Turns, you sit facing each other and take it in turns to be speaker or listener and to an agreed time period – say two minutes again. The speaker has two minutes to talk on any subject of their choice and their only job is to keep talking. The listener's job is to make it clear that they are both listening to and taking in what is being said. They do this by echoing back to the speaker what has been said. So, instead of just nodding or making sounds of agreement as the listener did in Taking Turns, this time the listener re-states what has been said to them. The listener can use the speaker's words or their own, but 'Reflective listening' isn't just being a parrot, it's rephrasing and checking out. This means you don't have to get it completely right the first time or every time – the speaker will correct you and it still works. The intention is for the listener to listen to and hear what the speaker is saying, not to put their own words into the speaker's mouth. It will sound a lot stranger to the person doing the reflective listening than to the speaker, so you might need some useful phrases to put in front of your mirrored speech. These could be 'It sounds as if you're saying . . . ', 'I imagine you're feeling . . . ', 'It seems to me that what you're saying is . . . ', 'What I hear you saying is . . . ', 'So, you're saying . . . ', 'So, let me get this right . . . ', 'If I can just check this out . . . '.

As with Taking Turns, you should try this out a few times, each time talking over how you both felt. For example, what was it like to have to hang on to the other's every word so that you could repeat them back with accuracy? And what was it like to have your words repeated back at you? Having your own words fed back at you not only gives you the chance to hear what you've said and clarify it, but makes you feel confident that you have been listened to and understood. As with Taking Turns it can seem a bit odd and awkward at first, but you could both get used to it. Whether you may use it to find your relationship could be mended, or whether you use it to cope better with a break-up and make any later relationship easier doesn't matter; knowing how to communicate with a partner will enrich your life.

Chapter Three
IF IT'S OVER

There are two basic and extreme approaches to the breakdown of a relationship. One is that if it isn't working it should go out on the rubbish heap with the other trash as soon as possible. This is perhaps the attitude increasingly shown in modern, industrial consumer societies in which everything becomes outmoded within a season. The second, and usually seen as the more traditional approach, is that relationships, particularly those formalised in marriage, should be saved at any cost. Whether you see your own relationship in either of these poles-apart beliefs or somewhere in-between mostly relates to how you've developed your sense of what makes a relationship and a family. Whether you throw up your hands and walk away at the first hint of trouble or stick it out through thick and thin even if your partner is a user and abuser, may depend on the pressures and support you feel from those around you.

PRESSURES

When a relationship begins to crumble there are many pressures either to shatter or maintain it. There are, for instance, the expectations that society as a whole has of separation and being separated, divorce and being divorced. It is true there is far, far less of a stigma attached to having been in a permanent relationship and leaving it nowadays, than there might have been last century, but there is still a lingering question mark over people in that situation. Gone are the days when being separated or divorced meant you were a social outcast, but we still tend to feel that we may have failed and been inadequate, and having to answer 'Divorced' or 'Separated' when asked our marital status marks us out as losers. But the views of friends and family are just as influential. They may have strong beliefs either way. They may feel that leaving the relationship would be an intense source of shame and that all it would need to improve matters would be for each party to buck up and be a better partner. Or they may have been against the union from the beginning and be putting tremendous pressure to bear on getting rid of the offending party. Friends usually come down firmly on the side of their particular buddy. This may seem supportive but is often less so if their interpretation of backing you up is to go for broke and tell you to leave when you would rather be supported in bringing it back together. And last but not least would be your own fears and anxieties which may be pushing and pulling you in far from helpful directions. Your emotions may be one of the most important barriers to making your relationship work. What may be coming between you in the first place could be a fear of closeness and intimacy. Indeed, your terror of the pain of breaking up may be exactly what is making it difficult for you to be able to having a lasting relationship and so, perversely, make it more likely that you have to go through exactly what you dread. But it is fear of ending that often locks people into unhappy and destructive relationships. The relationship may really not be working but the two of you keep on in an increasingly bitter non-relationship rather than go through a parting.

IF THERE ARE CHILDREN

If you have children the situation becomes even more complicated. If you are trying to decide whether it is better to stay together, even if this is not a satisfactory relationship, children put a terrible weight on the scales. Certain sections of the Press and certain politicians still feel it necessary to denounce single mothers at every opportunity. Single mothers are seen by some as the root of all society's ills – no-one seems to blame the missing men who are the other side of the equation. But whether publicly blamed or not, most men in a relationship that is coming apart at the seams do feel concern about the children. This means that anyone wrestling with doubts about breaking up a family will be aware of what the person left with the kids may be taking on. Knowing that some people will look down on them is one problem, but the hardest element to bear is the fear that social judgement might be right. From the letters I receive I know that many people are terrified that if they split their family, either leaving or throwing out the other parent, or being the one to leave their children behind, it dooms their kids to failure and delinquency.

Deciding to break up can also be hugely difficult if you've reached middle or old age. You may be frightened of being alone, thinking that at your time of life you'd have little chance of finding a new partner. You may be scared of managing on your own and feel that even an abusive or violent partner is better than no partner at all. If your children are adult, able to cope with their own lives and perhaps having families of their own, you may feel they would be particularly shocked and dis-appointed if their parents separated, just at the point when they felt you would settle down into respectable retirement. You may have specific worries about money, especially if the bulk of your income is from a retirement fund set up from one person's working life.

When it comes down to it, however much you may be left with intense feelings of failure and loss if a relationship ends, splitting up may be better than the alternative. Living with someone you don't love and who doesn't love you, can be the most damaging experience possible. It can be a brutal-ising experience. It can lead to total loss of self-esteem and confidence, it can lead to both parties becoming careless of the other's feelings, to becoming angry, cruel and even violent. When couples preserve an institution, that of their relationship, over their emotional well-being, the price is often not only their own happiness but their own humanity. When it is suggested that a family remain together even when the adults are no longer in harmony, what is often forgotten is the effect this disharmony has on everyone around them. Children who grow up in a family at war receive a thorough grounding in how to be miserable. The image they get of relationships is that partners belittle and degrade each other and hurt each other. Children from such families often say they will never get married. Whether they marry or not is irrelevant, they do naturally go on to have long-term relationships and these so often follow the pattern that they have observed in their own parents. So, 'Staying together for the sake of the children' far from giving children something positive to emulate does more damage than a separation ever would have done.

But let's look at it from the other side because there is really nothing quite as *potentially* damaging for a child as having their parents split up. If you ask children for their feelings on the matter while their parents are in conflict they will almost always say that staying together would be better than splitting up. What children fear more than anything else is loss – loss of a parent, loss of the sense that all is right with the world – which happens when a family breaks down. Children may often speak of the relief of no longer witnessing rows and fights and that the fact that their parents may be more settled and happy when a separation has occurred. But even when the parent who has left might have treated them unhappily or unfairly, children still feel that something vital is missing when their parents break up.

It is when parents separate that the big difference in what you need and what the children need occurs. In effect what you often have is a split situation – what may be good for you would be bad for the children, and the other way round. What is necessary for the break to leave you emotionally intact and able to move on is an ending. We need to draw a clear line under that relationship and bring it to a close. Now, that doesn't always mean never seeing each other again and pretending that the relationship never existed. On the contrary, being in touch as friends is often a sign of having been able to separate with no unfinished business. And wiping someone with whom you shared your life and your love out of the picture is not only difficult, it's dishonest and harmful. Couples who divide up their lives and their friends and who try and make sure that nothing that touches the other ever again touches them may truly be cutting off their own noses to spite their faces. You harm yourself just as much as you might harm your partner, but most important you don't help yourself finish and move on by being this radical.

THE SUM OF THE PARTS

The person you are and the person you will take into a new relationship are the result of all your experiences to date. Trying to pretend that an important aspect of your life never existed or is certainly no longer a part of your life is just asking for trouble. Apart from anything else you won't learn from the mistakes you might have made if you won't admit they ever happened. But more sadly, you will lose all the good times that were there in trying to reframe the experience as wholly bad and wholly to be removed. When you have children, trying to cut or airbrush your ex out of the picture becomes an even more damaging exercise. It is possible, of course, which is why it seems so appealing. This is, after all, a person you met and fell in love with some years into your life. They

occupy a percentage, not the whole, of your history and however damagingly they can be removed. But look at it from a
child's point of view. Your partner is their parent, someone
who has been there for 100 per cent of their existence. If your
children were yours by birth, genetically speaking, they con-
sist of half of you and half of them. While you are trying to cut
this person loose from you, you are doing it to the person who
is fully half of their body and perhaps of their personality. Even
if yours is an adopted or an assisted birth, this other person
may have hooks into your life which can be detached – they
have roots into your children's life that will cause something
to wither and die if you dig them up. You can end this other
person's involvement in your life; your children cannot. And
the messages you are giving about any desire to rid yourself of
this other person can only raise anxieties in them about themselves. If you hate their other parent so much, if you want to
remove their other parent so thoroughly, what about those
aspects of the other parent in them? Will you still love them, or
will you want to get rid of them in the same way? Or will the
price of love and security with you, be having to rid themselves
of anything in them that has links with the other parent?

Making an ending is horribly complicated when there are
children. You have to balance their needs with yours. You
have to finish emotionally with your ex while at the same time,
for their wellbeing, you need to continue to enable their on-
going relationship. You have to balance your recognition that
the links between you are no longer working with making sure
the links between them do. In a sense, you have to become
positively schizophrenic, splitting your approach to this other
person as a partner and as a parent. As a partner you have to
make a clear and clean ending. As a parent, you need to go
on having a relationship. Many of the difficulties we have
in couple relationships after a break down arise because of
problems in managing this split.

RUNAWAY FEELINGS

It's not easy to take a structured and logical approach to relationships. What is often very hard in these circumstances is to be able to look at what is going on, to ask ourselves what we would need to do to cause the least damage to everyone concerned and to act on what our answers may be. What actually happens is that we allow our feelings to run away with us. We may feel intense rage or intense yearning towards the other person and continue to act on that, come what may. Barry's actions, for instance, were extreme but demonstrated what may sometimes happen when people allow their profound feelings of anger to spill over into the way they behave.

Barry separated from his wife when she finally went to a solicitor after fifteen years of marriage. She obtained a court order barring him from the home because of his violence to her and towards the children. Barry found it extremely hard to take responsibility for his actions, insisting that he 'Only hit her when she deserved it, and the children needed disciplining as they were out of control'. Barry attempted to win a residency order which was turned down when all four children, aged thirteen, eleven, nine and eight, made it clear they were frightened of him and far preferred to stay with their mother. He was given visitation rights but broke arrangements time after time. He finally told his wife that he'd regain contact with his children when they were old enough to see his view of the story and be on his side. About six months after his last contact, his wife and children began to suffer from a 'hate' campaign by three families in the neighbourhood. The children were bullied both in school and out. Barry's by then ex-wife, had her house vandalised. She found many of her friends and acquaintances in the small town in which she lived were being told all sorts of scandalous stories about her behaviour which she traced back to these three families, all of

whom were friends of Barry's. While she had a court order forbidding him from approaching except at specific times, she
found it difficult to get help against these other people. She
finally wrote to Barry pointing out that if he wanted their
children to understand his point of view, making their lives a
total hell was not the way to go about it. She received no reply
and the bullying of her and her children persisted until she
finally, at great expense and terrible upheaval to the family,
moved away.

In order to make a good enough ending you do need to put
all sorts of things into all sorts of different compartments. You
may need to put your children's needs in one and yours in
another and recognise that you aren't going to manage to fulfil the wishes of both. Your children may desire you to stay a
family when you know that for your own wellbeing, and perhaps theirs, this isn't possible. It's especially not possible when
the reality is that what your children actually want is not for
you to stay together but for you to turn back time and return
to the way you were before your relationship came apart. But
you also need to put parts of your own needs and wishes into
different compartments as well. You have to separate your
hopes and dreams of what might have been, from an honest
look at what your relationship is now. But above all you will
need to separate out your anger and disappointment at what
your relationship might have become from your memories of
what it once was.

TOTAL DISMISSAL

Many people feel that the best way of dealing with the end of
a relationship is totally to dismiss it. A clean break is seen as
necessarily a clean break from the past as well as the present.
We try to rewrite history, to reframe the whole thing as a total

mistake from beginning to end, in order to ease its passing. Family and friends will often engage in this with a will, telling you that they never thought it would last, that they never liked your partner anyway, that they always had suspicions it would come to a sad end. What actually happens if you do this is that you are left with far more lingering doubts and hurts than if you remembered the good times. If it was always a mistake, what does that say about your judgement? You chose this other person, you stayed with them and now you are saying you were wrong. Doesn't that suggest that you can't trust your own judgement and that you may indeed make the same mistake all over again without knowing it? The total rejection option involves rejecting something of yourself. It's hurtful and damaging to your children, but it's also hurtful and damaging to yourself. But separate things out and you can deal with the apparent contradiction that involves accepting that it was once good and no longer is.

It's a strange fact that we change our minds all the time and yet live in a society that appears to insist on consistency. Politicians will swear against all the evidence, going through extraordinary contortions to insist, that what they are saying today was what they said last year. We seem to fear that there is something dreadfully wrong in being able to say 'I've looked at the evidence, things may now be different and I've changed my mind'. In real life what happens is that we change, and our circumstances change. What was right for us once may cease to be so. The person you loved and admired at sixteen may have fitted your blueprint then but ceases to do so when you are eighteen or 28. You change, they change and there is no longer the same meeting of minds and needs as there was. But the fact that you no longer fulfil or satisfy each other five, ten or fifteen years down the line does not alter the fact that once upon a time your heart beat at the very thought of them. Far from hindering you to finish, remembering past happiness actually helps you make a good ending. By recalling the good times, you balance up any feelings of failure and the sense that it was all such a waste of time. You reassure yourself that you made a good relationship even though it may now have gone sour. Accepting this gives you the confidence and the courage to know that you'll be able to make good relationships again.

HIGHS AND LOWS

However foolish it might make you feel or however unnecessary it may seem, making a point of both recalling the good times and putting the bad ones to rest can help end a relationship on a constructive note. Just as we need ceremonies and rituals to mark the high points in our life they are often necessary to get us through the low points as well. What a ceremony such as a wedding or a baptism does, is mark a change. It allows us to recognise that something will be different in our lives. The event carries us through the transition from, for instance, being a single person to the committed state of being one half of a couple. Or from a couple to being a family with children. We also have funerals to mark the closure of our relationship with someone who has died, an event where one can say goodbye and recognise that they are gone. But what we don't have are rituals that allow us to deal or come to terms with the ending of a relationship and to mark the transition from being a couple to being separate individuals again or from a family that lives together to being a family that lives apart. It would help if we did.

MARKING THE END

Taking part in an Ending Event may be a good way of helping you, and your friends and family, cope with the end of your relationship. Preparing for it – making it a ritual, or just an informal get-together – can help you come to terms with the fact that the ending has happened. Going through with such an event can help you acknowledge both the finish of something and the beginning of something else. Facing up to an end in such a definite way can help you move on. It can be an occasion for tears but also help you smile and remember happiness, and affirm that you will both smile and feel happiness again. You may want to do this on your own. But you may find that the person you are parting from and your wider family and friends may like to try this to mark the end of your relationship and ease you, and them, into the new phase of your life.

You may want to create and organise you own event or ritual, but you could start by recalling the good times in your relationship and thanking your partner, in memory or in the flesh, for them. You could remember and talk about what first attracted you to them and the experiences and feelings you shared. You could concentrate particularly on the elements of this that are lasting and that you will continue to treasure and cherish. If your partner is there, they could do the same. Each may tell the other what they would like to carry on from the relationship and what they hope the other person will remember and take with them. If you have children, you can reflect on the fact that even though the relationship as partners is over, you are still both parents to them. You could thank each other for your children and reassure them that you love them. If you are doing this together, each of you could take turns and if family or friends are present they may say something too. You may then consider the fact that you are parting and acknowledge the fact that your relationship has come to an end. Do this frankly but without bitterness or blame. If you are doing this as a couple or with your family you may then embrace and say goodbye.

Whether you do it on your own or as a couple with or without other participants, an ending ceremony is undoubtedly useful. You can make it a full ritual with candles that you may blow out at the appropriate moment to signify the extinguishing of the flame between you and you could toast each other as a way of wishing the other well on their future journey without you. You may like to write down the details of the positive things you want to remember and on a separate piece of paper record your affirmation that it is over. You may wish to keep the first as a way of hanging on to those good things and to tear up or throw away or burn the second as a way of marking that your relationship is finished.

GETTING STUCK

It's very easy to get stuck in a bad relationship and not to see a way out. If you were to be transported suddenly from the high point of your relationship, when you felt loved and wanted and were enjoying each other's company, to the low point when you may feel rejected, insecure, lacking in self-confidence and self-esteem, you would realise that something was very wrong. You would probably conclude that this was no way to live and take steps to insist on a change or to remove yourself forthwith. But, of course, that's not how it happens. Sometimes, violence or infidelity seems to blow up out of the blue and seems to be a total surprise. In most relationships that come to an end there is a gradual slide from satisfaction to dissatisfaction and both parties constantly reassure themselves that this is only temporary. Because the change is gradual, people tend to lose control over what is happening and how they may react to it, and feel powerless to effect any change. Often both parties have constant hope that the conflict or unhappiness will resolve. By the time you wake up and realise you are in a state of war you may be overwhelmed with feelings that sap your will and drain your energy. When a relationship fails people feel that it is they who are failures. You look around you at a society in which love and coupledom seem to be the norm and feel that you must be to blame for not being like everyone else. Couples may find themselves stuck in an intensely unhappy relationship convinced for various reasons that they cannot break out of it or indeed change it.

Bernice, for instance, wrote to me at her wit's end. She said her husband came home only to eat his evening meal after work and would then go out to pubs and clubs with his friends. Three or four times a week he would stay out overnight and would tell her it was none of her business where he was or who he was with. If she became upset or persisted in asking he would lose his temper and shout and sometimes hit her. But Bernice was absolutely certain that the one thing she couldn't do was end the marriage because she couldn't face the thought of having to bring up their three children alone. The house was comfortable and at least he paid the bills and, she said, living in a tiny flat would be more than she could bear. She also felt that she couldn't deprive the children of their father by taking them away. Jason was similarly sure that he needed to stick by his marriage. He and his wife never talked, she preferred spending time with her friends than with him and they hadn't shared a bedroom for five years. Yet he considered the costs of a separation and the reduced circumstances it would lead to, weighed more heavily than the continual and continued drain on his sense of self-worth at their staying together. Once he had made the break Jason could look back appalled at the unhappiness he and his wife had endured. Of course they were less well off at first – both had to make do with small houses instead of the big one they had lived in together. And Jason clearly appeared to have less contact with his children since he no longer lived with them and saw them

at weekends and two evenings a week. But even these drawbacks actually ironed out in time. Jason's now ex-wife went
back to full-time work and eventually earned enough to get
a better home. Jason re-partnered and so did she. Since
Jason and his children made more effort to be in touch their
relationship actually improved. But the most important
change was that both Jason and his ex-wife realised that
their reasons for putting off the split had more to do with the
emotional pain of parting than any genuine impossibility.
Once they had faced up to the fact that it was over they found
that seeing it as impossible was actually the biggest barrier of
all, far bigger than money or contact issues between parents
and children.

FOR THE SAKE OF THE CHILDREN . . .

All the evidence seems to suggest that simply staying together
for the sake of the children is not a happy option. Continuing
in an unhappy and possibly bitter relationship gives children
a devastatingly destructive lesson about relationships. This
could colour their ability to make happy relationships later in
life. It's important to recognise that your interests and their
wishes may differ, and to accept that sometimes you may have
to make a choice with which your children disagree. It's
counterproductive to stay in misery, thinking that continuing
the outward appearance of a relationship would be good for
them. But for your children's sake, you may want to make
efforts to try to repair your relationship before seeking to
dissolve it. And if you decide that separation is necessary
you have a responsibility to them as well as yourselves to
make that ending as good as possible. It is not separation itself
that gives children a bad start in life. If you compare the
four groups: children whose parents stayed together happily;

those whose parents stayed together unhappily; those whose parents separated with acrimony; and those whose parents separated with civility, the first and the last have outcomes that are fairly close. The worst off were those whose parents separated in bitterness, with those whose parents stayed together unhappily not much better. Of course children from a happy family fare the best, but children whose parents break asunder but manage that break sensitively seem to suffer little lasting harm. It's the manner of your separation, not the fact that you separated, that damages both you and any children you have. If your relationship has come to an end, you can't turn back the clock. You have to accept you're now working with the 'given' of a broken relationship and it's no use trying to sink your head in the sand and wish for everything to be as it was. What you can do is go on, and make the best of it.

We often find it hard to admit that a relationship is ending because doing so means letting some very uncomfortable feelings out of the box. It's not just that being in love and happy with someone makes us feel secure, wanted and needed. We also have expectations about relationships that are to do with status, both in the eyes of the world and our friends and in our own eyes. Having a good relationship is a measure of success, so some people may feel not having one is a measure of failure. And having had one and lost it can be seen as the biggest failure of all. So if you look squarely at the fact that your relationship is ending you may have to let well up the pain and loss of losing love, the disappointment of having the future you might have planned taken from you, the sadness of having your dreams dashed. You may also have the anger and bitterness towards your partner for the part they may have played in the relationship not working, but there will also be intense guilt and shame for what you may feel you have or have not done. Most acutely of all there may be a feeling of failure – not just at having failed but of *being* a failure. Admitting to an ending may admit to all this. No wonder the temptation is to keep it all under wraps, to keep saying 'Tomorrow is another day' and to carry on turning your face away from what may be obvious to everyone around you; that this is a relationship with no future. The harsh truth is that not only do you need to face up to these feelings, you have to experience and go through them in order to come out at the other side.

NO EASY WAY OUT

There is no easy or gentle way to make an ending. A common query to agony pages is one such as Carys's who wrote 'I've fallen in love with a wonderful man. The problem is that we are both married and both have children. We've been seeing each other for two years and now realise we simply can't go on like this. We have to be together. I don't love my husband any more but I'm still fond of him and the man I love feels the same about his wife. We don't want to hurt them nor do we want to upset our families, so how can we leave them and be together without causing them any pain?' The sad answer is that you cannot end a relationship without someone feeling pain. It's simply not an option. And the sad thing is that in trying to make it easier, far worse hurts are often inflicted. Many terrible crimes are committed in the name of 'Being kind'. Husbands will give their wives and family one last Christmas, one last wedding anniversary, one last holiday in the belief that carrying on as normal through these will somehow soften the blow. The experience in fact produces infinitely more misery. Most often, the behaviour of the person about to leave signals clearly the fact that they may be physically present but are emotionally absent. There's no enjoyment to be had at all because what is coming is obvious to everyone, even though no-one wants to bring it out into the open. Even if when the leave-taking is announced it comes as a total surprise, it ruins the experience in retrospect. Many a child, many an adult, has had their enjoyment of family holidays or Christmas or birthdays tainted for all time because it becomes the anniversary of that ending. When you give in to making love one last time, to staying with your partner through one particular crisis or another, one particular event or another, the feelings you are saving are not theirs but your own. If it's over it's over, don't prolong the agony.

TIPS FOR MOVING ON

Every change and adjustment requires that you cope, and coping is exhausting. If you're going to move forward and break up without breaking down, you need to find ways to work your way through this journey effectively. Here are some suggestions that should help you to emphasise your strengths, deal with any weaknesses and boost your self-esteem and confidence:

• You may find yourself looking back and regretting some of the choices and decisions you've made. When this happens, allow yourself to mourn the things you've lost but let go. Don't see it as having lost opportunities; see it as having taken one path among many, and realise there are more ways than one of getting from A to B. Address your regrets by focusing on what you *can* do *now*, and in the future. Instead of wasting time and energy on looking back, look forward and set yourself new goals. If you need to make changes to achieve them, that's where your energy should be concentrated.

- Take control. If you feel realistically in control of your life, you'll feel happier and healthier. Self-esteem, self-confidence, self-worth and the knowledge you can do it, all rely on your being in the driving seat. It's very easy to grow up with the feeling that life happens to us, that events just occur and that being in charge of our own lives is beyond our grasp. This isn't true. If you allow yourself to be directed by what other people expect of you or steered by what life tosses your way, the fact is that you're choosing to be helpless and pushed around. You can choose to be the one having the say on what you do and what you feel. Just *do it*.

You can feel the satisfaction of being in charge if you begin to:

- Become clear about what's most important to you. Keep your sights set on your goals. Don't let other people's demands, or even your own belief that there are things you have to do, distract you. Kath, for instance, decided she wanted to recover from years of having abusive relationships and being a victim. She decided she wanted a home of her own, a responsible job and a loving relationship. She found a good job, but moaned to her friends that she was sure she wouldn't be able to cope. She looked for an apartment, but every time she found one she liked, would listen to her mother's criticisms – it was too small, too big, in the wrong area. When she met someone at work she really liked, she cancelled several dates with him, arguing that she had work or other commitments that had to be done at that very time. Kath finally faced up to the fact that she was taking her eye off the ball; she was letting her fears and insecurities come between her and what she really wanted.

- Delegate. You can't do everything yourself, so don't try. Accept help and ask for it from those close to you. You'll get a lot more done, with less stress. You'll also feel better about your relationships with friends and family because you won't feel angry, let down or resentful.

- Focus on what you do well. Take 'time out' to think about all the things you do and all the things you've done. Having a clear sense of what you can do gives you the confidence you need to get through what may well be a difficult period. If you think you could brush up on your skills, find a way. There are plenty of people and organisations who can teach you skills and help you use them. Kath felt she was disorganised and incompetent, which was why she was terrified her new boss would 'find her out' and get rid of her. When she sat down to work out what she was good at doing, she realised she'd had years of being the person in a relationship who actually got on and did the work. All the men she'd been with not only mucked her around, they'd also left her to struggle with too little money and too many responsibilities. Without realising it she'd become a skilled manager, accountant and negotiator – she just hadn't put such labels on her skills. Kath spoke to her boss about her feelings of being under-skilled. Not only did her boss reassure and encourage Kath, but she sent her on courses that allowed Kath to recognise, polish and increase the abilities she already had.

- As well as knowing what you can do, accept what you can't. This can enable you to plan for events that are likely to occur but go with the flow when you do come up against disappointments and events beyond your control. Kath realised she couldn't stop her mother being critical, nor her ex-husband being as careless about their son's feelings as he had been of hers. She couldn't be the perfect daughter her mother seemed to demand nor protect her son from realising his father wasn't the perfect father. All she could

be was herself – and that she could accept that was good
enough.

- Take some time every day to be in the moment. Close your
eyes, let everything outside yourself fade into the background and listen to your own breathing for a few moments.
Put aside your worries and let all the things you may need
to do wait. Just float. Listen to your breathing, think about
something peaceful such as waves gently rippling on a
sandy beach or clouds drifting in the sky.

- Do some regular exercise. It can be vigorous walking,
cycling or running, step or aerobics, or weight training.
(If you haven't done any exercise for some time or have any
health concerns, have a word with your doctor or practice
nurse first.) Physical activity reduces stress and increases
well-being, both physical and psychological. Developing
good lifestyle habits will help you have the time to make
your most important dreams come true.

- Make friends, keep friends and stay in touch with family. A
network of deep, caring and supportive relationships feels
good and helps you stay healthy. You need people around
you who know you in all the different roles you have – as a
friend, a daughter or son, a parent, a work-mate. Being
alone and unsupported leads to more than loneliness – it
can actually increase your chances of suffering ill-health.

You are important. You may need to recognise this in order to
get the courage to make a break from a relationship that is
doing you harm. Or you may need to accept it to recover from
the pain of having been left by an ex-partner. The Personal Bill
of Rights is one way of affirming your rights, to Life, Liberty
and Happiness. You might like to copy this out and stick it
somewhere prominent – on your fridge door or by the phone –
to remind yourself when you're feeling low.

Personal Bill of Rights

---

1. I have the right to ask for what I want
2. I have the right to say no to requests or demands I can't meet
3. I have the right to express all of my feelings, positive or negative
4. I have the right to change my mind
5. I have the right to make mistakes and not have to be perfect
6. I have the right to follow my own values and standards
7. I have the right to say no to anything when I feel I am not ready, it is unsafe or it violates my own values
8. I have the right to determine my own priorities
9. I have the right *not* to be responsible for other's behaviour, actions, feelings or problems
10. I have the right to expect honesty from others
11. I have the right to be angry at someone I love
12. I have the right to be uniquely myself
13. I have the right to feel scared and say 'I'm afraid'
14. I have the right to say 'I don't know'
15. I have the right to not give excuses or reasons for my behaviour or refusal to do something
16. I have the right to make decisions based on my feelings
17. I have the right to my own needs for personal space and time
18. I have the right to be playful and frivolous
19. I have the right to be healthier than those around me
20. I have the right to live in a non-abusive environment
21. I have the right to make friends and be comfortable around people
22. I have the right to change and grow
23. I have the right to have my needs and wants respected by others
24. I have the right to be treated with dignity and respect
25. I have the right to be happy

Chapter Four
A FRESH START?

On the face of it a relationship where there are no children is much easier to end. Not only are the issues much clearer since you have only your own feelings to consider but you can make a clean break. Where there are children there will always be a link between you and your ex-partner through your kids. The fact is that your children share genes with both you and this other person. Even if you lose touch this means that they remain a figure, however distant and shadowy, in their lives. And if they figure in your children's lives, they do so in yours too. So, if the relationship is not working and you don't have the glue of children holding you together, what stops you walking away? The reality is that children don't always hold a couple together and their absence doesn't always make it easier to come apart. What is true, however, is that if you don't have a shared stake in the future through children it is often that much easier once a relationship has ended to feel that the best way to cope with the sadness and loss is to wipe it off the face of the earth.

Couples who separate when there aren't any children often opt for erasure rather than an ending. They see the best way of going forward is to reject utterly not just the other person but everything that went with them. When Ally and Jethro divorced, both left the area in which they'd lived together for two years. They lost contact with the friends they'd had together, got new jobs, new friends and new interests. Ally not only threw away all the photographs that showed Jethro or her and Jethro, she dumped everything – photos, shared belongings, souvenirs of holidays – that came from their time together. When Mark separated from Dan who had been his partner of seven years, he did much the same. They had a shared interest in cycling and met when they both went on a biking holiday in France. Throughout their relationship most of their holidays were spent cycle touring, in Europe and once in the States. They spent many weekends on their own as a couple or with friends mountain biking. They split up in anger and bitterness. Although the relationship had been rocky for some time, it all came to a head when Mark had an affair. Most of their friends were horrified and disappointed in Mark and sympathetic to Dan and many of them refused to talk to Mark. Mark's way of handling the ending was to walk out, abandoning not only many of his possessions but also their shared life. He took up running as an alternative form of exercise and steadfastly turned his back on something that had been central to himself and his life for over ten years.

A THREAD TO THE FUTURE

Even without children, if you've shared your life with another person, you create a thread that continues on into your future. You may not be together but what you had as a couple influences what you continue to be on your own. You don't have a choice about this. The only choice you have is whether you are going to be in or out of control of how it affects you and whether the influence will be negative or productive. If you try and wipe out the person and what they meant to you, you will be turning your back on elements of yourself. Mark, for instance, allowed his bitterness to rule. By avoiding cycling he lost something he enjoyed. He lost the memories of the fun he, and they, had had by trying to remove any chance of being reminded of any guilt or pain that he felt.

Even trying to erase memories of unhappy or destructive experiences can turn on you. Petra divorced her husband after five years of a violent marriage. She was determined to cut all ties with him, his family, their friends and indeed her own family who she saw, quite correctly, as all being part of her abuse. Both families had a pattern of abusive relationships and two serious boyfriends she had had before marrying had also been violent. Petra persuaded herself that the only way to deal with it was to get away and forget about the lot of them. She asked her firm to relocate her, took further training and was promoted into a better job. Two years later she remarried and a year after that found herself yet again under the threat of violence. In turning her back on her past Petra had refused to consider why she might have chosen the particular relationships she had and why this pattern may repeat. In refusing to think about it, she just got stuck into doing it all over again. Petra was all ready to make a clean break and a fresh start again except that her new husband Lee, who was also on his second marriage, insisted on going to counselling.

You can make a clean break and a fresh start without having to deny or reject either the relationship, what drew you to the other person, what happened with them or what you might carry over into the rest of your life. What is behind you is a foundation for what is in front of you. You may want to dismantle your relationship but you can't entirely eradicate it and pretending you can do so is really only like sweeping something under a carpet. The bumps and lumps are likely to trip you up or to fester into a pretty mean mass that's going to make itself known as it oozes out. Trying to turn your back entirely also means denying things you'd perhaps want to

retain. Just as Mark lost his cycling you may find yourself
losing Paris in the Spring, or that particular red wine you used
to share, or the joy of picnics in the park. Not only may you
want to turn your back on shared experiences, you may also
lose shared friends.

FRIENDS

Friends may make themselves scarce when a relationship ends
for many reasons. Friends often split along fault lines. If
you went into a relationship with separate friends you may
find you come out with those intact. But friends you made as
a couple may divide themselves into two camps or back off
altogether. Some people will take up the cause of the person
they see as their particular ally. It's often on the lines of same-
sex, so women will back up the woman of the couple, and men
will be behind the man. But frequently couples will gravitate
towards the person they feel a particular bond with or who
they think is in the right. This isn't always helpful. If you are
trying to heal the relationship between you in order to end on
a constructive note it can be distracting and downright
dangerous to have friends who are spoiling for a fight or
who think the best way of supporting you is to run the
other person down, and cut them dead. But what often sadly
happens is that separation is seen as rather frightening,
depressing and 'catching'. Friends whose own relationships
may be a little unstable will want to avoid you. Your misery
raises anxieties in themselves and maybe points out the
uncertainties in their own lives. The opposite-sex partner in a
relationship may not want to have any more contact in case
you give their own partner ideas, and the same-sex may want
you out of the way in case you make a play or are played
for by their partner. (Of course, if you're gay, if you have

straight friends read same-sex and then opposite-sex in that sentence!)

One of the most difficult balancing acts is in dealing with members of your soon to be ex-partner's family. In the main they will see their role as backing up their relative and so be antagonistic towards you. If there is no need to keep a balance because there aren't children's feelings to consider this may evolve into full-scale war or rejection. This can be particularly painful if you've been fond of and have had a good relationship with in-laws.

A 'GOOD ENOUGH' ENDING

So how do you cope with ending a relationship without ending everything else that came with it? You need to aim for integration rather than disintegration, to embrace what you had in order to go on to a new future. A 'good enough' ending involves drawing a line under the past. It doesn't mean you should try and rip it up and pretend it was never there. If you've faced up to what happened and why, if you've experienced your sadness, you don't have to throw everything out in order not to feel pain. Mark had to get rid of his cycling because any suggestion of it brought him face to face with his guilt about why they broke up. His coping technique was to avoid what happened and why, which in the end was far more destructive than facing up to it.

RITUALS

We all tend to mark changes and transitions in our lives with rituals. Many of these are obvious and conscious, such as the formal ceremony of a wedding or funeral or the party or celebration that accompanies a silver wedding anniversary or 21st birthday. But there are other ceremonies we indulge in often without recognising the significance. When a relationship breaks up, for instance, women frequently change their hairstyle and buy clothes that are more colourful, sexier and younger in style than they may have been used to wearing recently. The reason for this may be a boost for self-esteem and self-confidence with the reassurance that they are still attractive and vital. It also has the practical advantage of acting as a signal to other people that they are back on the market, single and fancy-free once again. Men may return to behaviour they had in the days before they had a permanent relationship, going to clubs and bars on their own or with male friends. This behaviour may follow a separation as a way of almost defiantly showing to the world that they have come through a period of turmoil and discomfort. But it may also happen while the couple are still together, in the last days of a failing romance. Then, it's a warning signal and an often unconscious recognition that not only is something not right in the relationship but that it is actually drawing to a close.

One way of setting yourself up for a fresh start, a new beginning, is deliberately to construct a ritual for yourself. The aim will be to do something to set yourself off on your new life. We've already looked at an ending ritual that closes and finishes the relationship you had. Ending rituals take both people and their affect on each other into account. This, however will be something that is about you and you alone, to symbolise and make real your entry into the next phase of your life. You may choose this to be a change in your appearance. Having your hair cut in a dramatically different style is effective for both men and women. A new article of clothing, even if it's just a pair of socks, can be used to state emphatically to yourself and to other people that you are dressing up a new you. You might choose to start looking after yourself in a different way by enrolling in a regular fitness class or sport or by taking up walking or running. You may begin treating yourself each day with an hour of something that really pleases you such as locking the bathroom door and taking a long relaxing bath or forbidding anyone to interrupt while you relax and listen to some music. You may go on a new diet – not a short bout of crash starvation but a total over-haul of your daily eating so that from this point onwards you eat more fresh fruit and vegetables, less fat and empty calo-ries. You may decide this is the opportunity you've needed to get yourself some more training or a better job. Some of these are small changes that occur at one particular point in time and that just say 'This marks a transition from one period in my life to another'. You may wish to do it simply by toasting yourself in a glass of fruit juice or alcohol, and saying 'Here's to the future, a new day and a new me!' Some of the others are more radical alterations that not only register that something has happened but that actually allow you to make a change in your life for the better. But however you do it, it really does help to let yourself recognise that you are passing from one era to another. Seizing control in this way can often stop you slid-ing into depression following what has happened and allow you to set the tone for the future.

'GOOD THINGS' AND 'BAD THINGS'

You may also need to focus on elements of your past life with your previous partner in order to be able to pick out the bits you want to discard and the bits you want to retain. One way of doing this is to cherry pick.

Cherry Picking

Sit down with some paper and a pen and divide it into two columns. Label one side 'Good things' and write down everything that comes to your mind that was good about or in your relationship or in your life before it. You might find yourself putting down activities you shared such as going to the pub, visiting car boot sales on a Sunday, watching golf matches, eating certain ethnic dishes, going to Italy on holiday. Be honest with yourself and put down everything even if the memory makes you weep and causes pain. Now fill in the side labelled 'Bad things'. You might want to record the way you argued, the way you might have been stopped from doing things you enjoyed by a partner who didn't share these interests. Doing this exercise may be painful and provoke bitterness or tears but grit your teeth and do it. Then look at the two lists and draw up a new sheet, this time with only one column. On this put down only positives, but positives you culled from both good things and bad things. What you list are all the things you would like to retain or reclaim from your previous life. If you enjoyed collecting Elvis memorabilia with your previous partner, don't deny yourself that pleasure simply because it reminds you of them and ultimately of the bad parts of your relationship. Reframe it as not only a celebration of the good elements but as a way of reasserting the fact that you have the right to continue owning behaviour that gave you pleasure. Of course, if you were involved in expending time, effort and money and only did it for their sake, you may want to happily and defiantly discard it and find yourself something that can truly be your own. If you think that something you really enjoyed, such as Paris in the springtime, will always be tainted by unhappy memories of the end of your relationship, make a commitment to win it back for yourself. Arrange to go to the place or do the activity with a supportive friend or family member. Expect it to be sad and difficult and for there to be tears or even anger. Allow these emotions to come out and you will find that they wash over you and pass. Give yourself permission to experience them and you will find that they fade, leaving you with that place or that activity back in the zone of your control and enjoyment. If there are aspects in the 'Bad things' column that you would like to turn around, enter the positive statement or commitment on your list that deals with them. If, for instance, you've remembered the fact that you and your partner were prone to getting into circular arguments, make a commitment to learn how to argue more constructively. If there was something that you stopped or were stopped from doing during your relationship, a type of activity such as playing squash, or going on a type of holiday such as sightseeing because your partner preferred lounging on the beach, then commit yourself to finally doing it.

REVISITING

You may find that there were things you used to do, people you used to see that have gone by the board during your relationship. Now you have only yourself to please one way of making your single state positive would be to revisit these. It's not unusual to have lost touch or even to have argued with people who were once important to you when you began the relationship that has just ended or during it. Sometimes this happens because you and your partner do develop together along lines that were different to the ones you took before. Sometimes losing touch happens because your partner actively attempted to isolate you or bind you to themselves. Sometimes the parting of the ways with friends or family came about because of your partner's jealousy, fear or possessiveness. However irrevocable you feel this may have been it's always worth making the effort to make contact again. Perhaps the most effective way of doing this is to write a note or a letter. You don't need to go into tortuous apologies or explanations. You simply need to say that you have been thinking of them and have missed being in touch, that the separation was something that happened during your relationship that you regretted and that now you and your ex-partner are no longer together you would very much like to see or talk to them again. Acknowledge that they may feel disappointed or angry at what happened and hope that this will not prevent a new beginning.

You may feel that the best way of making a fresh start is to sever all connection with both aspects of yourself in the past, and your past partner. Even if you do accept that it would be far healthier and constructive to retain links with what the past meant to you, maybe it's far harder to accept the idea of remaining in touch with the ex-partner. You may feel angry and bitter or hurt and disappointed in them and in what you felt they did to you. Or you may feel embarrassed and disappointed in the way you felt you behaved and not wish to face them again. Even if there are no reasons for you to ever see each other again, if there are no children to form a link, it may still be difficult and ultimately painful to totally avoid each other. If you still work together, for instance, it may not only be hard for you, but difficult for your colleagues to maintain a fiction that the other does not exist. If you live in a small town, trying to avoid each other may put you to unnecessary bother. And, of course, if you have friends in common it makes it really difficult for them having to ensure that they divide their time between you with no clashes, no embarrassment and no hurt. Facing up to endings and getting it all out into the open may help you to move on to being at least on Christmas-card terms. By this, I mean able to be in touch and to exchange cordial wishes for each other's wellbeing and mean it. So, how can you arrive at a state of mind that allows you to move on, with confidence? What you will have to do is plan for the future and make a resolution to move on.

Every New Year, most of us make resolutions. We promise ourselves that we're going to do something different – give up smoking, diet, do some exercise. The one constant element in all our promises is that we want to change, either our lives or ourselves. Sometimes the promises are realistic, sometimes they are totally unreasonable. Sometimes we keep them, sometimes we do not. The end of a relationship and the start of a new life should and could give you the opportunity not only to make new resolutions, but to find ways of making them work for you.

MAKING CHANGES

Change is always difficult. We often wish our lives and our relationships would stand still, or go back to being as they were, when it seemed simpler and better. The hard fact of life, however, is that nothing can stand still. To make a new and fresh start, then, we have to make a transition. A transition is the process we go through, the bridge that takes us from one state of mind, one type of life, to another. Learning how to manage a transition allows us to choose change when we're stuck in a situation that causes pain and holds us back.

To begin a change, you have to let go. You may need to let go of people, of emotions, of what you were and even what you hoped to become. Even good changes means letting go of something. Even if you made a change, such as moving to a new home or a new job that you've chosen and looked forward to, you'd still find it confusing, tiring and often depressing. When the changes are forced upon you or come out of an upsetting situation such as the end of a relationship, the disorienting feelings will be worse. But you can thrive in transition, too, even when it begins beyond your control and out of your hands. Following are some ways that may help.

Mourn

Identify what you are losing. It can be the person from whom you're separating, the lifestyle you had with them, your belief that all was right with the world; most likely, it's a combination of these and other things, people, feelings. When you have an idea of what you feel is going, acknowledge that losing it will be difficult and painful. Then, mourn your losses. Cry, scream, howl at the moon; punch pillows, throw china and tear up tissues. Expect to feel anxious, miserable, confused, depressed and angry. Feel it. Then get over it.

Picture it

Picture yourself having come through, at the end of the process you're only just starting. Ask yourself 'What would my life be like if I got what I wanted?' Start off by fantasising winning the lottery and getting off with a film or rock star – be over-the-top and totally impractical. Then, come a little – but only a little – down to earth. Think of a life you could have in your grasp, with time, effort, imagination. Picture it, and you living in it. Now, let's see how you can do it.

Make your cunning plan

You're at Stage One and your plan is to get to Stage Two. It may seem a very long and almost impossible journey, and it would be unworkable if you thought you could only do it by jumping from A to Z in one move. So the trick is to break it down in small, manageable, steps. Realise what you're trying to do is go from A to B, not A to Z. Write down all the things you want to be different. Describe the present situation and how it would be if it had changed. Then imagine tiny, bit-by-bit stages that would take you from one to the other. Brainstorm solutions to your problems. This means writing down everything that comes to mind without weighing up whether it is reasonable or can work, until you've finished your list. Sometimes the crazy idea you'd have thrown out, turns out to be the best. By the end, instead of having an impossible task which you'd only succeed at with a magic wand, what you should have is a shopping list of action points which may take some time, but can be achieved. Patience and persistence are the key.

Be flexible

Remind yourself that the plan isn't written in stone. Expect to run into unforeseen hazards and be flexible. Accept that you will need to tinker about to find what works, so see everything as an experiment. Sooner or later you'll find what works, and it may not be first-time lucky. When you do come up against a setback and any disappointments, tell yourself that this is a temporary hold-up, not a total derailment. There is no such thing as failure. Every stumble along your way is a learning experience – a result that gives you important information. Instead of blaming yourself and taking it as a sign of failure, ask yourself what you can learn from this, pick yourself up and stride on. See life as a game to be played, not a test to be taken. And you may find you don't get exactly the end solution you wanted in the beginning, so learn to see the journey as being as least as important as the destination. You may not get to where you wanted to go, but if you've opened yourself up to new ideas and learned to look at yourself in creative ways, where you get to may be even better. Do as well as you can and then let go.

Don't take it personally

Keep reminding yourself you deserve to have the life you want. You deserve to be loved, to be successful, to be valued. Realise that whatever has happened to you in the past isn't to do with you – it isn't because you are unworthy, unlovable or in any way at fault.

Separate acts from people

You may tell yourself that you hate, are angry at, loathe and despise the person from whom you are separating. Doubtless, you do and are! But the problem with directing all these negative feelings at a person, is that you can't then disentangle them from what they did or what happened. Instead of being the person you fell in love with – the person capable of making your heart sing and your blood surge – they become a monster who destroyed your happiness, your life. It may feel satisfying to direct all the hate and locate all the badness in them, but it actually doesn't help you move on. And it doesn't help you learn to make better relationships later on. So it is important to separate acts from people. Focus on recognising that this was a person you once loved who has done things that you hate, that hurt, that led to your parting; what you are angry, hurt about and perhaps despise, is what they did, not what they are. That way, you can retain the memory of how you were happy with them before it all went wrong.

Feel it

Be prepared to be scared. It's a natural part of change and comes with the territory. You're not being weak or stupid to be on an emotional roller coaster, and to feel like screaming, crying or laughing at a moment's notice. This also means you have every right to express fear and anger, pain and loneliness, as well as delight and joy, lust and love.

Build on what you have

At a time when you're overhauling your life and may be making grand and sweeping changes, keep your foundations. Have a think about the things you don't want to change and need to stay as they are. This is a part of your life that is coming to an end, not your whole life, and elements of your life you would like to change, not all of it. Write down all the constant and steady parts of your life – the people and rela-tionships, the things, the favourite pursuits – that you want to keep. Build on these.

Learn from the past

Cast your mind back to other times when you've had to pass from one stage in your life to another. Was it hard or easy, did you feel you coped or not? What helped or hindered you, what could have made a difference? How can you use those lessons to make it easier now?

Give yourself a boost

Do something you know you enjoy and do well. Make it some-thing short and sweet, so you can see results quickly. Bake a cake, write a poem, mend a fence, plant a flower – anything as long as it gives you a sense of satisfaction, completion and accomplishment. This will put you in a winning frame of mind. Hold the feeling and remind yourself that this is how it's going to feel when you achieve the things you've planned to do. It will also show you that you *can* achieve, you are capable and competent and you will succeed.

Network

You're not the only one making a change in life. There will be plenty of other people going through exactly the same situation; and plenty more making different changes but having the same feelings. Join up and thrash over your emotions and how you're coping. Find them through friends, family, specialist support groups (see Useful addresses, page 181).

Look after yourself

Find a treat that makes you feel loved and cared for, special and important. It may be doing yoga or meditation, it may be taking half an hour in the morning or night to have a long, relaxing bath. It may be having ten minutes to do some gardening, an afternoon walking the dog, an evening doing some reading. Whatever it is, make time in your week, every week, for your time to look after yourself.

Chapter Five

WHAT DO YOU TELL THE CHILDREN?

'We couldn't face telling our son we were getting divorced. We were having terrible arguments for months and he asked a few times if we were alright. One of his friends at school had parents who split up and I think he was worried we would too, but I'm sorry to say I fobbed him off and said everything would be fine. Then we stopped arguing, because we stopped talking. He didn't ask again and we didn't say anything. I think we both just kept hoping it would get better so there never seemed a good time to tell him. It wasn't until Paul actually moved out that we finally told him it was happening. That was five years ago and I don't think he's ever forgiven us for keeping him in the dark. I'm always asking him how he feels and what he's doing but he doesn't let on much and I know he doesn't come to either of us with his worries.'

When you have kids, the end of a relationship can be more than just painful. You can't help feeling you've failed, even if you're sure your partner was to blame. And notions of fault and blame only muddy the water, making a difficult situation impossible. If you have only yourself to think about, you may find the decision-making around taking your leave of this relationship hard enough; if and when to go, what to say, who to tell? If you have children, their confusion and hurt can compound your guilt and anger, making you hesitate and delay even more. Your children may cause you to have second (and third and fourth) thoughts about what you would like to do over your relationship. What their existence may certainly do is give you sleepless nights over what and when you tell them that your relationship is in trouble or ending.

CHILDREN BECOME INVISIBLE

Frequently, couples who are having problems become so wrapped up in their own misery that it's as if their children become invisible. You now they're there, you know they are involved, you know they have or will have feelings about what is going on in their family, but all this gets pushed to the side. Sometimes, you're just so upset you simply forget to think about their impressions, feelings and needs. More often, you convince yourselves that children don't notice, are happier being reassured and better off being shielded from your worry and sadness. Sadly, this simply isn't true. Kids aren't stupid and will usually realise there are problems, and have their own fears and worries about what they see in the family. The longer you put off being honest the harder it may be for you to tell them, and for them ever to trust you again.

All families alter at some time or other. In a sense, a separation or divorce is just another type of family change; perhaps one that seems a bit more drastic and painful than some others, but similar in many ways. A new family member being born, an old one dying or new experiences such as starting school, going to a secondary school, moving house, will all produce ripples of influence that are just as potentially damaging and confusing as a separation. Some children and some families bounce back and cope with family change. What makes the difference between those that do and those that do not isn't the situation in itself, but how you approach it and how you deal with it. What makes a difference to your family is not its structure – whether you are a family of two parents living together, or living apart – but what happens within the family and between parents and children before, during and after a split.

You and your children have a fundamental difference in your relationship to your partner. This is that you choose a partner, but you're landed with your parents. This may be a small and simple difference but it has profound consequences. It means that while you can unchoose, they cannot. You can decide to sever an emotional link and no longer be married to or living with a partner. Whatever they may feel about this person and wherever they may live, children cannot turn their backs on a lasting attachment. This also means a fundamental difference in approach. An adult may put up with a bad and even an abusive relationship for far too long. This may be because of religious principles that tell you a marriage is for life. Or it may be because you're frightened that if you leave this relationship, no-one else will have you. You may feel so lacking in self-confidence and self-esteem that you feel this is the only relationship, or type of relationship, you deserve. Whatever your reasons, at the back of your mind will still be the fact that you can debate the issue; that there is the possibility of leaving and you're only arguing if, how, what, why and when. And, of course, if your partner has been the one to leave, what you're discussing is how to cope. But, the bottom line is that for you or your partner, as adults, leaving is a choice that can be made. Children don't choose to leave their parents. They may sometimes run away or act in ways that appear to reject their parents, if what has been going on in the home is so painful that they can't cope. But this is almost always an appeal for help. What young people rarely do is walk away from the parental relationship, as adults can and do walk away from a partner relationship and, indeed, a parental one.

This is why the balance of how and what you tell your children is such a delicate one. Your children share genes with both of you. In fact, even if their genetic make-up isn't half and half – if they were assisted conceptions, for instance, born by donor insemination or with a donor egg and the male partner's sperm or are adopted – if they have known you as their parents for a significant part of their lives, they will feel that half of themselves come from each parent. This has greater consequences than simply feeling pulled in half when you argue or divide. When you are angry at or criticise your partner, their parent, they feel it's levelled at them too. If you hate, or are disgusted by, or fear your partner, they will fear that your feelings towards that half they carry inside themselves will be the same as the feelings you are expressing or demonstrating towards their other parent. And, indeed, if you are telling them that your partner is wicked, evil, irredeemably awful, they may conclude that this means you think the same about them.

ADULTS CHOOSE, CHILDREN ARE LANDED

There is a narrow line between covering up and thus lying about your feelings and spilling it all out in such a way as to alarm them and make them feel responsible. Children do need to see your sadness and even your anger and frustration. Trying to keep too in control gives them the impression you don't care or that feelings are dangerous things that have to be kept under the covers. Honesty is important when breaking the news to children that the family is about to change. Of course, to be honest with your children you may first have to be honest with yourself. Parents often deny to their children that anything is wrong in their relationships because it is they who want to believe this is so. If you *are* trying, together, to mend your marriage, you can tell them that you are doing your best to solve the difficulties. But if the truth is that your relationship is at an end, it really only hurts them more to delay the moment they have to realise this. All children of split families will have fantasies about their parents getting back together again. Right up to and beyond a parent remarrying and even having a new child with another partner, children will dream of their mum and dad reuniting. Delaying the truth only feeds these dreams and leaves them more disillusioned.

You do, however, need to balance being honest and telling them what happened, with not bad-mouthing the other parent. You may need to tell the truth at some point. Shakeela left her husband Marc when their son, Simon, was four. Marc had been violent and unfaithful, but Shakeela simply explained that they had stopped loving each other and never ran Marc down to their son. When Simon was ten, Shakeela discovered that Marc had been telling Simon that the divorce was all Shakeela's fault, saying that she had had a string of affairs and would scream and hit him. Shakeela was faced with the dilemma of whether to set the record straight and if so, how. She had avoided telling him about his father's infidelity and violence because she thought it would confuse and depress him. She hadn't wanted him to have divided loyalties or feel a person he loved had behaved badly to another person he loved. But now she was worried. Marc had never hit Simon but she wondered if, having started to show anger towards her in front of him, Marc may move on to hitting his son too. She eventually sat down with Simon and said 'I know Dad's been saying some things about why we split up. It must be quite painful for you to hear these things. What did you feel about this?' Simon became tearful and angry, blaming

Shakeela and saying she was an awful mother do have done this. So Shakeela said 'You know, when people break up they can be angry and guilty and sometimes they're not always honest about what happened. I've never said anything bad about your Dad because he's your Dad and you love him. I'm sad he's saying nasty things about me.' Simon then asked her 'Were you seeing other men, then?' 'No, Simon, I wasn't.' 'Dad said you'd scream and shout at him.' 'Yes, I did. I was very angry at some of the things I felt he was doing.' 'What was he doing?' 'That's between him and me and I don't think it right to talk to you about it.' Simon thought a few minutes and then asked 'So is Dad lying?' 'I think your Dad loves you and is still upset at the break-up. He wants you to love him and perhaps he thinks if you're angry with me, you'll love him more, and be on his side.' 'That's silly'. 'I think you can love us both without having to blame either of us. Why we split up has nothing to do with you and should stay between us. But if your Dad ever does anything to hurt or frighten you, you should know it's not your fault or because of anything you've done, so speak to me about it.' Shakeela wrote to Marc saying she didn't want to get into an argument about who did what but that he was upsetting Simon. She said that if he was try-ing to win Simon over, it was having the opposite effect and maybe he should think about that. Marc stopped, but sadly Simon said he didn't want to see his father as often as he had been.

TELLING THE CHILDREN

When you tell your children your relationship is in trouble and may be ending, you need to keep three things clearly in your mind. The first is not to confuse honesty with being inappro-priate. Children need to hear the truth from you and need to be

able both to ask questions and have their own feelings
appreciated and heard. They need to know what has happened
and why and what is going to happen and why. They need
to know the unadorned truth and not lies or fantasy. They
need to be reassured. But the things they emphatically do
not need or want, are to be used or abused and caught in the
crossfire.

What shouldn't happen is for them to feel responsible for
your feelings, either for the existence of them or solving them.
Your children, even when they are grown-up, are your children.
They are not your best friends, 'like a sister or brother' or as
adult as you. You may think that they are big enough to support you and are capable of being leaned on, but it's positively
damaging to your child to have to 'parent' his or her own
parent. Leaning on or relying on your kids and telling them
that they have to look after their brothers or sisters or you, or
that it's their role now to 'be the man/woman of the house'
leads to confusion and difficulty in making relationships later
in life. Ben's father left when he was twelve, and both his
grandmother and his mother went to great pains to tell him
that he was now The Man of the House. This had various
results. Ben became very competent and mature, doing chores
and getting a Saturday job to bring in some money. He had
always got on well with his younger brother and sister however, and that changed. Both resented the way he now told
them what to do – 'bossed them around' as they saw it. His
schoolwork suffered, because he would come home early on the
days his mother was upset or feeling unable to cope. And,
having Ben to look after her, this happened a lot. When Ben
was fifteen, his mother met a man and it looked for some time
as if she would remarry. It came to nothing, mostly because
Ben and he clashed and argued bitterly. This was hardly
surprising as Ben saw him as a rival and resented having to
give up his place as both the first in his mother's affections,

and The Man of the House. Ben left school early and married at the age of nineteen, to a girl who leaned on him heavily. Four years later, the marriage was in trouble, for two reasons. She suddenly decided she wanted to stand on her own two feet, go back to college and get some qualifications. And she also resented his mother's continual demands on Ben – it seemed she couldn't change a light bulb or go to the shops without his help, advice or presence, and he still saw her every day, usually dropping in for a cup of tea on the way home from work.

USING THE CHILD AS 'AMMUNITION'

It's very easy to use children not just to back you up or shore you up but also to carry on the argument with your partner. In the run up to a separation children often find themselves being used as the glue that tries to hold the family together. You or your partner may, for instance, have left the relationship in all but name. There may be an affair going on, or one of you may be emotionally absent even while still living in the shared home. But you may use your children as your excuse, to yourself or others, for not taking the final step. A common statement heard by agony aunts and counsellors of all sorts from their clients is 'I would leave today but my children are in the middle of exams/at a delicate age/having a hard time at the moment'. Whether this is an expression of genuine concern, or a good excuse for inaction, the result is the same; the child carries the can and becomes aware that they are in the middle of a war zone. Children also frequently become the means by which an argument is carried out. Parents may stop standing side-by-side on child-care issues and be drawn to taking contrasting and opposing views on both important and trivial details. This means they can stop arguing about all the things to do with their own relationship – money, love and sex – and carry on the rows over their kids – homework, discipline, friends, the hours they should be coming in or going to bed. This not only puts a child under tremendous strain it also make him or her feel entirely responsible for the continuance of their family. If all the rows seem to be about them, they quickly feel to blame for the break-up of their family.

Telling a child that you are breaking up and giving them some idea as to why this is happening is not the same as confiding the intimate details of your relationship or its coming apart. To do so would be to tell them altogether too much about your private relationship. All children have hopes and desires about their place in the family and their importance to each parent. They want to be told that they are the most important person in your lives, the one you love best. It's quite true that children do often entertain the sneaky wish that mum or dad would vanish and they would be installed in their place. A young child will often tell dad or mum 'When I grow up, I'm going to marry you' and such a fantasy is normal and common. But if a parent actually does leave, and the child is told too much or relied on too much, the outcome is far from pleasurable for the child. The results can be very destructive. They may feel guilt and terror at what they see as the power of their wishes and dreams. They may find themselves locked in a pattern of relationship with you that is difficult to break afterwards. They may feel unable to leave home and make their own relationships. After all, they may feel, since it was their secret and guilty desires that got rid of their rival and left them in control, they cannot in turn desert the parent. A child who has been told that they have to take the place of the missing parent may dramatically resent any new partner you later wish to bring in. And if you don't make any other relationships, the child may be overcome with anxiety or guilt and feel responsible for your being alone, and responsible for your care for ever more, even when they get to the stage when they should be making their own relationships.

IT WON'T BE A SURPRISE

The second detail to keep in mind when considering what to tell them is not to assume that this is a total surprise. However well you may have thought you had hidden your disagreements or unhappiness, children aren't stupid. They are hardly likely to have let it go completely over their heads. They genuinely may not have realised the situation was bad enough to be approaching a split. This is more likely, as you might have been working very hard at denying that their worst fears might be realised. But if you assume that they have been in blissful ignorance you pass on several rather unhelpful messages. It would be as if you were telling them not to trust their instincts. They know something is wrong, and yet here are the people they most love and trust in all the world saying that they shouldn't have realised there has been a change. By assuming ignorance, you also tell them that deceit and silence are expected within your family. In effect you lay down the lesson that questions are not to be raised and that anxieties are to be suppressed. The result may well be that if they have worries and problems in the future they know not to raise them with you at an early stage because in your family bad things are to be ignored until the very last moment.

You may not want to tell your children that your relationship is in trouble until you are sure that it is. This is fair enough; you don't have to make announcements about your own feelings or your own plans, but do at least tackle your children's worries. You can, when problems begin to bother you, ask them what may worry or upset them and deal with it up-front. A vital aspect to keep in mind, however, is to do this without giving false reassurances or making promises you can't keep. So if for instance a child says 'You are arguing a lot. Are you going to get a divorce?' you could say 'We are having a few problems and we are not very happy at the moment. We are doing our best to make it better but we want you to know that we love you very much and will always be your mum and dad'.

BAD PARTNER – GOOD PARENT

However upset you may feel about your partner, and however bad a partner you may think they have been to you, the fact is that this doesn't necessarily make them a bad parent. They may have fallen short up to now, but may at least come good for their children if given the chance. If you present the situation to your children as a one-sided, Good versus Evil picture, you may sabotage your partner's ability to do so. So it's important to be able to divide your feelings about their behaviour to you, from any feelings about their behaviour or responsibilities to your children. That also means separating what you feel about their behaviour, from what you feel about them. You may be furious at the person from whom you are separating. It may feel satisfying to blame them and tell your children it's all their fault, but if you do, it's your children who will suffer most. Focus on recognising that this was a person you once loved, who is the other parent of your children, who has done things that you hate, that hurt, that led to your part-ing; but what you are angry and hurt about, and perhaps despise, is what they did, not what they are. That way, you can keep hold of the fact that your children have every reason to love you both, support you both, and keep in touch with you both.

MORE THAN ONCE

An equally important factor is not to see this as a one-off declaration. Having made the announcement that you are about to
part, don't feel that you no longer need to discuss the matter
again with your children. Parents often take the same line with
that other taboo, sex, and think that a one-off lecture settles the
matter for once and for all. Your children will need to revisit
what you have said again and again. Even teenagers need to
go over it, repeatedly. Young children may want to go back to
the subject even more. They will need to know what it means
to you and what it means for them. They will need to rehash
the same areas repeatedly and to go on and develop them.
However painful or difficult it may be for you it's important to
recognise that just as an ending can't be wrapped up and dis-
posed of in one short burst of activity, just as a relationship
cannot be consigned to history and forgotten about, so how
you deal with it with your children may need to be slowly and
with repetition.

As mentioned earlier, separating parents often imagine that
they have managed to keep from their children the pain and
worry of knowing what is going on. Some parents fall into the
trap of believing that they protect their children from hurt by
keeping it secret until the last moment. This is possibly the
worst choice you can make. They'll know there are problems,
so keeping quiet only teaches them that you are capable of
lying and can't be trusted. The longer you put off being honest with them, the more they know that you are the last people
to ever approach with a problem that needs discussing. It is
true that kids will frequently assume that whatever they experience is 'normal'. Don't all mums and dads scream and shout
at each other? Don't all mums or dads sometimes spend nights
away from home? Don't all parents sometimes live apart? The
point is that even very young children will recognise what is

happening in their family, they simply may not have the language or the experience to ask about or discuss it. They may be worried, but unable to put their worries into words. What they can understand is anger, loss, and a lack of love. What they can't understand is why it's happening. But just because they can't or won't say anything, doesn't mean they don't feel it.

Just as it's important to keep your kids out of the rows, and not ask them to take sides, it helps to tell them together that you are parting. When you know it's all over, get together on this and discuss what you are going to say. Pick a moment when the two of you are calm. You can explain, even to very young children, what you are going to do. Sit down and offer a lap to sit on, arms to hug. Tell them that mum and dad will no longer be together. Stress that while you can't be partners you'll always be parents, and ask them to tell you what they feel and what they would like to tell you about this. If one or both of you isn't going to be able to overcome your anger or your tears, tell your children on your own. What you can say, with truth, is that the other one, deep down, does love them but finds it difficult to show it. And stress that none of what has happened or will happen is the child's fault or responsibility. If you already have a plan for separating – who is going, where and when – tell them. If you don't, say you'll let them know as soon as you do.

MIXED REACTIONS

Expect mixed reactions. There may be some relief, that arguments and uncertainty are over – in some families, there may be a good deal of relief. They may tell you they're glad you've come to a decision. But however upsetting it's been to live with unhappy and even violent parents, some children may cling to the idea of their family staying together. They may argue, heatedly and tearfully, against a split. Some may feel a terrible loss, and may even blame themselves, and ask if they behaved better and were good, whether that might mean you stayed as a family. However, children frequently keep their emotions hidden and may seem surprisingly 'don't care' about the whole thing. They may say nothing and refuse to talk about it. It's easy to see why you may get the idea they don't understand, simply to accept your assurances that everything will be OK. But they often do mind, desperately, which is why they may ignore it all, hoping it will all go away if they do. Keeping talking to them and acknowledging that they probably find it frightening and hard is important. When they're ready, they'll open up. You may be startled to find them shrugging, not asking questions and just kicking their heels until you let them go back to whatever they were doing when you asked them to come and listen to you. But they'll feel it, and soon show their emotions in action.

Young people tend to take out their anger and pain on themselves, or on everyone else. Younger children, and some older ones, go back to childish behaviour, doing all the things they may have left behind several years before. They may revert to wetting beds, having tantrums, sulking, crying, complaining, being 'difficult'. This is more than likely in the under tens but can happen even in older children. They may refuse to go to school, or sneak off and play truant. They may become hostile and withdrawn, aggressive and unfriendly. They may become bullies, or begin to be the target of bullies. They may start dropping friends or neglecting schoolwork or turn their back on things they once enjoyed. Teens may dabble in early sex and destructive activity such as stealing, joyriding, vandalism or fighting. Or they may become involved in self-destructive activity such as drug-taking or even self-harm such as cutting themselves.

LISTEN, LISTEN, LISTEN

Deal with it all by recognising they're trying to say 'Listen to me, I'm in pain!' and give them the comfort they need. Make the time to talk with them and listen to what they have to say. Just as parents often believe keeping quiet and pretending everything is fine can help, so we also often feel that playing down a young person's fears will reassure them. So when a child expresses anxiety, worry or dismay, we tell them not to be silly and not to concern themselves. Far from being helpful, this can leave a child even more scared and unsure. When a doctor tells a child 'This isn't going to hurt' and then sticks a big needle in them that makes them scream, the child learns i) that adults lie ii) that adults don't know what they're talking about and iii) that if it wasn't supposed to hurt and it did, that must have been because of something the child did wrong and it's their fault. Telling a child not to worry when it would be natural for them to do so, or that their fears are silly, has the same effect. They learn that you lie, can't be trusted, don't understand – or that they themselves are bad, incompetent, foolish, unlovable, worthless people. Listening and saying 'I can see why you feel that' or 'It's natural to feel like that' doesn't undermine you, doesn't increase their fears and doesn't open a Pandora's Box of other problems. Accept their anxieties and then talk to them about how you all may improve matters.

The most reassuring news is that studies show children aren't harmed by the fact their parents separated; what does the damage is how you split and how you manage being parents who live apart. So stop blaming yourselves for what you can't help – which is the fact you are separating – and put some effort into what you can help – which is how you are helping your kids deal with that fact. Above all, make sure both of you continue to be caring parents, however you feel about each other.

Tips for Telling

- Put your anger aside to work out how you'll continue to both be parents. You can stop being partners but you can never give up being a parent. You may be parting but your children deserve and need *both* parents.
- Just because your relationship or their family has failed, it doesn't mean any of you are failures.
- Bad behaviour doesn't mean they are bad children – it's a common reaction to a break-up.
- Tell your kids what is happening as soon as possible and be honest with them.

Chapter Six

BLUEPRINT FOR A BREAK-UP

Your partner's left, or you've decided to leave them. The break-up is about to happen, or it's happened, and you're finding the situation hard to deal with. The question that might be on your lips is 'If there has to be an ending, how do we do it as painlessly and as easily as possible?' We've already dealt, in Chapter One, with how break-ups usually happen. Let's now see how you might approach the situation, either before the event or even after.

When we talk about relationships ending we will often use phrases like 'breaking up' or 'separating'. This may describe how you actually feel about yourself during the process, that not only your relationship but you and your life are dis-integrating, shattering and coming apart. However, for all the violent finality of these words the reality is sometimes different. When relationships end people often don't detach from each other at all but remain linked, for months, years and sometimes for ever. This may be not just because you're both engaged in the constructive task of co-parenting any children, but because you remain bound together with the glue of anger and bitterness. The process itself can be long, drawn out and gradual, and go in fits and starts to an inconclusive end. You may feel overcome and overwhelmed, that everything you touch will crumble and that you aren't capable of managing at all. The good news, however, is that you have more strengths and more abilities than you recognise.

AFFAIRS

A typical cause of relationship break-up occurs when one partner finds someone else, falls in love, perhaps has an affair and it is this that comes between them. Much of the anger and pain felt by the betrayed partner will be directed towards the other man or woman, who is seen as the villain of the piece. All blame is attached to them, they are often cast in the role of seducer and destroyer of a relationship or a family. We frequently imagine that if they hadn't come on the scene, all would have been well. In fact, an affair is invariably a symptom of something that has already been going on in a relationship or with one of the partners. It's a delusion to think that someone has an affair simply because the opportunity presents itself or because they fall in love. People have affairs for a complex variety of reasons. One may be that they are terrified of commitment and that even if they have apparently settled down in a one-to-one relationship with another person they can't bring themselves to be truly intimate. Having an affair or affairs is a coping technique either to prevent themselves from being truly one-to-one or to throw a spanner in the works of the relationship, making it clear to the other partner that they are not the only one. Whether the affair is discovered or not, it serves as a barrier between the couple. The other and perhaps more common reason is that one partner looks for someone to lean on and satisfy needs when the relationship has gone downhill. There has already been an emotional parting of the ways when this other person comes on the scene.

Having an affair, however, is often an extremely effective strategy to avoid having to face up to an ending. The man or woman who goes straight from one bed to the next is effectively cushioning the blow. The whole situation may be messy, argumentative and bitter but, for them, it's not an ending, and that may be the point. Indeed, people who have endless affairs not only hold intimacy at bay they also make sure they never have to grieve a loss. As soon as one relationship draws to a close, or even as soon as it starts to get in trouble, they jump straight into another one. An affair may also be used as a way of shifting the responsibility for an ending so you don't have to suffer it. One partner may leave clues scattered all over the place pointing to the fact that there is someone else in their life. They may not have recognised what they are doing but the motive is to be caught. It's not that they want to hurt their partner, what they want is for the other one to have the burden of deciding to end it.

Much is stacked against you in trying to make a decent ending. You will be trying to protect yourself and all those around you from the anxieties and the hurt, and in doing so you may well be tending towards delaying, concealing, putting off. The truth is that however badly people behave, and however horribly they may hurt those around them it is hardly ever done with deliberate intent; it's not even done because they are unaware of, or don't care about, the pain they cause. People behave stupidly, viciously and damagingly simply because they are trying to hold off pain from themselves and in doing so everyone else gets caught in the backlash. Endings are best when both partners come together to agree it's over, to make their farewells and to co-operate on the separation. But if one partner is into avoidance, the other may still be able to bring their shared life to a conclusion on their own. However, you do need to recognise that you're doing this for yourself, by yourself.

ENDING AS WELL AS POSSIBLE

If you want to make an ending from which you and those around you can emerge as well as possible the first step is to accept that it simply can't be done painlessly. Fix that in your mind. It's going to be uncomfortable for you and it's going to be uncomfortable for everyone else and there is simply no way around this. But while there is absolutely no choice over the fact that people are going to feel hurt, you have a choice as to how much and how far. Leave it to chance and leave it to the end and the likelihood is that the situation will become messier and nastier. Take control and face up to your feelings, your needs, your responsibilities and your decisions squarely and while it may feel as if you are making it worse you will actually be making the situation infinitely better. In effect what you have to do is finish the business. Leaving unfinished business is what hurts.

If you avoid ending it between the two of you, you may never quite feel as if you've separated. You will find that when you do meet someone else you will keep being reminded of your ex and feel guilty and confused as if you were betraying them. If you start a relationship before fully separating you may find you can never fully commit to it, as the shadow of your ex hangs over you. Unfinished business can lead either or both of you continuing the argument between you, often for years. This may mean literally arguing, either by wrangling over property and belongings that you are still trying to split up, or through your children if you have them. Such arguments seem to be about the money, property, children – the excuse and the territory over which people squabble. In fact, they're really about an inability to let go. The antagonism continues because, deep down, the antagonists have never accepted and never recognised it's over. They feel they still have something to say, either because they've never managed to say it or because it's never been heard. People can continue the argument even if they never see or speak to each other again, by constantly recalling old arguments in their minds and going over what they wish they had said or should have said. Sadly, where this can lead you is to find yourself re-running the whole thing with a new partner. You may find your new relationship going exactly the same way as the old one. This may not only be because you choose a similar person and so find yourself in a similar situation, it can also be because when you are arguing with and shouting at your new partner it's the old one you are really talking to.

The message then is to finish the argument. By that I don't mean have a row or an endless series of rows with the other person; your partner, or ex-partner. I mean end the quarrel – finish it, have your say, put it to bed. Arguments can go on for ages and become circular, endless and futile because we don't end them.

CIRCULAR ARGUMENTS

Often the reason arguments become circular or don't end is that we don't feel that the other person has heard us and we are not listening to them. To bring any argument to a conclusion you need to feel heard and to take on board what the other person is feeling and saying. You finish the argument by going into this aiming not for a win but a draw. When we argue the problem lies in the fact that our goal is often to win the argument. We want to change the other person in some way, not just to have them see our point of view, but to have them alter their feelings, opinions and behaviour in line with our needs and wishes. Needless to say, the other person has the same goal in mind. You clash because both of you have mutually exclusive desires – to come out on top. If instead you set as your goal having the other person hear, accept, understand and acknowledge what you are feeling and saying, you have more chance of success. But to do so you need to offer that you will do the same.

FINISHING THE ARGUMENT

To finish the argument, make a suggestion to your partner that you meet at a time when both of you are feeling calm. Choose, also, a neutral spot. You can meet to talk by yourselves but it really does help to have a counsellor or a mediator to help you do it. Meeting in a counsellor's or mediator's office is useful because neither of you feels the other one has more control of the situation. Neither are you able to flounce out on the defensive or go on the offensive because of where you are. If you meet in the kitchen of your shared home, for instance, one of you may feel that this is their territory and the other that they are at a disadvantage because of this. Having someone else present also helps if one or both of you feel the other may get their way through physical threat or emotional bullying. But the most important aspect of having a neutral helper is that they can guide you in sticking to the point, discussing rather than fighting and getting it all said in as non-confrontational a way as possible. Agree from the beginning that the point of this discussion is to hear and be heard. Agree to sit down and talk and listen in turn, each having equal time – use a clock if you find this hard – and to go on until you've reached a mutually acceptable result. Agree that if the going gets painful or tough, you'll have a time out for ten minutes, an hour or even a day, but will return until both of you are satisfied.

FOUR STEPS

Seeing this as a four-step stairway to climb is a useful way of looking at the task you have ahead of you. To get your point across and break away from each other and your relationship, without continuing bitterness, you need to:

1 Work out what's making it difficult
2 Get the picture
3 Work out what you want to do
4 Do something about it

1 *Working out what's making it difficult*

Working out what's making it difficult requires concentration and effort. We often think we know not only what is wrong, but what is hindering us in dealing with an upsetting and difficult situation. We just as frequently concentrate our complaints, bitterness or anger on a red herring. For instance, you and a partner may be having arguments about whether you will split up, or who's going to leave and who's going to stay. You may be arguing, or winding up to arguing, about The Other Man (or Woman) if there is one, access to the children, money. You may feel you've come to the absolute end of any possibility of agreement, that there is no hope for reconciliation and that your partner is being totally unreasonable. You may see your only option as getting a solicitor to take them to the cleaners. But perhaps what you actually want isn't a legal fight but for the other person to notice you, to recognise what you once meant to each other, and an apology. In other words, your complaint may have been about what you feel your partner is doing – picking arguments, having an affair – when the real complaint is that you feel the relationship hasn't ended, there are all sorts of unanswered questions and loose threads hanging around and your partner simply isn't listening to you. You want to arrive at some solution, but you feel blocked and stuck. What may help is the following exercise, which is designed to focus on yourselves as a couple, either on your own or with the help of a counsellor, and to try and identify what may be preventing the two of you unblocking the situation and moving ahead.

If you can't agree to do this together, it still helps one of you, on your own. When a situation has become stuck, it's obviously better to address your problems together, but one of you can make a big difference alone. The reason for this is that it takes two to tango. If only one of you stops fighting and starts behaving in a different way, the other is actually forced to take up a new position. Look at it as being as if the two of you are balanced on a see-saw. Stay in your same positions, at opposite ends, and you remain balanced in a distant, hostile position. If you can agree, you both simultaneously move towards each other and the middle. But if one of you seems to refuse to move but the other moves on their own, the first person has to move too, to balance, or will fall off. If you both continue to argue and fight, the arguments get worse and the situation remains hostile. If one of you refuses to fight, the situation has to calm down. So even if your partner starts by refusing to consider, negotiate or discuss, do the work on your own. The chance are that sooner or later they may catch up and join in. And even if they don't, you'll have gained some control, of your feelings and the situation, and be able to cope better.

Say What You Feel

The real root of difficulties in any relationship is not actions but our feelings about actions. And what often hinders us coping with a break-up cleanly is that we get fixed in quarrelling about what the other person did, not what we felt. So instead of scooting off down the path of 'You did such-and-such' 'No I didn't !' 'Yes you did !', you would be better off concentrating on explaining how you feel, both to them and to yourself. People can always deny any charge you make about what they did. They can dispute that they did it, or maintain at least that that wasn't what they meant – and while they may be fooling themselves about the first, they could be perfectly truthful about the second. But there's no argument about what you felt. So, saying 'You had an affair and you're a beast' can be contested, while saying 'I really felt hurt and rejected' puts a whole new slant on things. When you sit down to talk to the other person, or when you sit down to plan on your own, make this rule; only say 'I feel . . . ' and ban yourself from saying, dwelling on or even thinking anything that begins with 'You . . . '. Sentences that rely on 'You make me . . . ' 'You did . . . ', 'You didn't . . . ' lead to conflict. Those that begin 'I feel . . . sorry/sad/upset/angry/rejected/cheated' or whatever, tend to lead to discussion. The aim is to put your point of view, not to criticise or attack. The whole point of the exercise is to confront your problems not the other person.

Own What You Say

While you're making the effort to put your feelings on the line instead of reproaching, you might also try 'owning' what you say. Promise yourself that everything you put forward has to be your own thoughts and feelings and you should acknowledge them as such. When we're being argumentative and hurt, it's very tempting to bring in our friends, parents, neighbours as witnesses or accusers. So we tend to try to share or evade responsibility for what we are saying by claiming 'So-and-so says' or 'Everyone knows'. So be clear that what you're talking about here is how *you* feel and think, and that the discussion is between you and the other person alone.

2 *Getting the picture*

In the middle of a break-up, you really are in a 'can't see the wood for the trees' situation. You may be so full of pain and fury that all you can concentrate on is the person in front of you and what has happened in the last few days, weeks or months. It often helps to widen your frame. Ask yourself 'When have I felt like this before?' You may discover one of the reasons the situation is so hard to deal with is that it does take you back to another rejection, another loss, long ago. Think back to the suggestions that have already been made about exploring your own past and even that of your family, to cast light on why you are in this particular relationship, having these particular problems. It isn't just you, or just the other person, and it isn't just now that has created this situation or your difficulties with it. Getting the picture is an important step to moving on. If you've made the picture a bit clearer you may be able to understand what has led to the two of you handling the break up in the ways you have.

3 *Working out what you want to do*

When you were a small child, the only way you knew to get what you wanted was by screaming, throwing yourself on the floor, throwing things, holding your breath until you got your way. Most of the time, of course, you got nothing of the sort. Even if you did win, the upshot was that you and everyone around you felt aggrieved and unhappy. The sad part of break-ups is that in the resultant break down, all those deep and unhappy feelings, throws most of us back to acting like toddlers. And we emerge feeling just as cheated or cheating as we did as screaming toddlers. There's nothing childish about those unhappy feelings, or about wanting to express them in this way. Expressing them by talking about them and by negotiating a solution often works better, however. It takes,

and needs, some effort to stick to this. And successful negotiation takes preparation, a willingness to listen and be flexible,
and a bit of time.

So do your homework. What do you want? Decide your bottom line; what you can't, won't go without. Link these with the
things you're prepared to offer in exchange for your must-
haves – the guarantees or concessions you'd be prepared to
offer your partner as a swap. You have to consider your partner's point of view and prepare your responses to any objections they may have, and your reply to any offers or requests
they may have or make. Prepare to be both reasonable and flexible – you can't expect all the bidding to go your way and you
may need to give a little to gain some. And don't forget that
both of you may start from what the other sees as an unreasonable position but may move towards the centre if you give
it time, patience and a willingness to stay at the negotiating
table long enough. Before you start, ask yourself what you'd set
as your 'Walk away' position. This is the agreement that gives
you the least points you want to gain. Be realistic about this but
once you've set it in your mind, walk away if you can't get that
much. But make it a walk away, not a flounce or run away.
Frame a 'No' as a 'Not yet and we'll keep talking'. The end aim
of this kind of discussion is to reach the point where you both
feel that you have been heard and appreciated. This means
there is no winner or loser, but an all-round agreement on the
outcome. To reach this point you have to ensure that neither
shouts the other down for what they say and that you discuss
all points rather than arguing with each other. Make sure that
you give yourself sufficient time for the exercise so that each of
you has the chance to have your full say.

4 *Doing something about it*

Once we are aware of the problem, and have worked out
what's wrong, why it's happened, and what we would like to

be different, actually putting it into practice can seem impossible. This is why breaking your moves down into small, manageable steps will be important. To do this, it really helps to think through all your anxieties, wishes and needs to come up with a plan of action. Getting all your ideas out in the open can be a great start.

FIRST THOUGHTS

Looking at your First Thoughts is an incredibly helpful and effective way of getting your wagons in a circle. When it all seems too confusing, when you seem to have too much to consider or can't come up with a single useful or workable idea, try this technique. Sit down with a paper and pen, or at your computer, and ask yourself The Question. You can use this technique to get problems into focus, or come up with a strategy to deal with them. The Question you might ask here would be 'What do I have to do to deal with this separation?' So what are the details you may have to consider? You may have to think about finances and their significance in your separation. How will you divide money, how will you manage? And how will you make sure arguments over money don't become an issue and a hook to keep you unwillingly tied together? If you have children, what will happen about contact for them? What about belongings – how are you going to split up your shared home? What will you do about any pets in your family? What about work – will one or both of you need to make new job arrangements? And what about childcare in the school holidays? How will you manage telling all your friends and family, and the necessary authorities that you are separating? When are you parting and how? Who lives where, and how are you arranging this? How will you deal with your feelings of loss and pain? How will you get back your self-esteem?

Ask the question and then write down *everything* that comes to mind. And I do mean Everything. If 'Cry for a year and a day' comes to mind, put it down. Write down even the crazy, unrealistic fantasies such as 'Run away to the Caribbean' or 'Put a contract out on my ex'. (Hey, that *is* crazy and unrealistic!) Among the silly and fantastical you will also put the practical, such as 'Learn to cook', 'Set up my own bank account', 'Tell the kids', 'Get home of my own', 'Give myself some treats'.

Once you've got your list, you can go through it. You'll be able to delete some (consign that contract killing to the Recycle Bin) but among the apparently silly you may find some that take a second look. 'Become Prime Minister so I can pass a law against all cheating partners', for instance! Well, why shouldn't you join a political party and work to have a say? Why not go back to college to train to do something to make your own and other people's lives different and better? Why not join a charity or group that works for and with parents?

DIY OR GET HELP?

You'll find your list falls into two main categories; things you can do for yourself and things you may need outside, professional assistance with. And it often does help, even with the things you're doing for yourself, to have someone to support, guide and back you up. You can see a counsellor face-to-face or access telephone support from organisations such as Parentline Plus for this. You can contact your local Citizens' Advice Bureau who are the best people to ask for any practical problems, such as worries about money, housing or legal matters. They or the National Debtline are particularly helpful on money worries. You may want to talk to a solicitor to help you through the legal details. I would strongly advise you to seek a solicitor through the Solicitors Family Law Association. They are committed to helping separating couples come together to agree. Unlike some lawyers, they won't rush you down the route of confrontation and conflict. Some solicitors offer a short interview that allows you enough time to get a lot of questions answered for a fixed fee of as little as £10. Some even offer surgeries with a one-off free interview. Your local Citizens' Advice Bureau will know who offers these services in your area. If you are married, you may want to consider how you will divorce – by mutual agreement after two years, or by suing for adultery or unreasonable behaviour. If you're not married, you may still need a solicitor to help you over the details of dividing a shared home, and shared finances and, if you have children, discussing and agreeing how you may deal in the future with your shared responsibilities.

FLOWCHART

When you're left with a list that sounds right, you can put each point in some sort of order of importance. You can then do a 'flow chart' of what has to be done first to allow you to move on to another point. Break everything down into small, manageable, attainable steps. You can't expect to leap from being a couple to being on your own, from being in floods of tears of grief or anger to being calm, collected and organised in a day, in one smooth jump. Accept that you may need to fall back one move for every advance of two. Even if you stumble back several steps, a gradual movement forwards is progress. Make a point of picking one, little thing you know you can do from your list each week. You'll then be able to pat yourself on the back for having done it to completion. And you can cheat by making it very small and very easy!

LOOK AFTER YOURSELF

While you're in the process of breaking up, and recovering from this, you may feel like someone going through and then recuperating from a nasty illness. You'll feel physically sick at times, weak and ailing. You'll be in need of Tender Loving Care, but may be wrapped up in looking after other people with no-one to care for you. It's really important that you recognise that you need and deserve care, too. And that you take the time and effort to give yourself as much help as you are offering other people. So take this advice to heart:

- Be gentle with yourself!
- Remind yourself you are not a magician. You can't work miracles.
- Find a hermit spot. Use it daily.
- Give support, encouragement and praise. Learn to accept it in return.
- Change your routines often and your tasks when you can.
- Learn to recognise the difference between complaining that off-loads and makes you feel better, and complaining that just reinforces stress.
- Focus on one good thing that happened today.
- Schedule 'withdraw' periods at least twice a week when you can be calm and at peace and no-one interrupts you.
- Say 'I choose' rather than 'I should' or 'I ought to' or 'I have to' or 'I must'.
- Say 'I won't' rather than 'I can't'.
- Say NO sometimes – you can't do everything. If you never say NO, what is your YES worth?
- Admit you can't cope if you're having trouble and ask for help. Trying to manage on your own can be seen as being aloof, distant or indifferent and this is far more hurtful and harmful to those who love you than telling them you need a hand.
- Allow yourself to have fun.

Chapter Seven
IF IT TURNS UGLY

There is often destructive bitterness and even explosive anger felt and expressed around a break-up. But sometimes this emerges in more than just a raised voice or a slammed door. Anger is one thing, and can be painful and difficult to deal with whether you're feeling it or coping with a partner who is feeling it and expressing it to – or at – you. Violence, however, is quite another matter. While all endings are painful and difficult, some relationships and partners make a break-up particularly risky and unpleasant. Both men and women can react to a partner telling them 'It's over' with rage that can spiral out of control and fantasies of revenge that can be made real. We may laugh at stories of spurned wives and husbands pouring paint over cars, cutting the sleeves off clothes and distributing the contents of a prized wine cellar about the village; we may joke about angry, deserted women being 'bunny boilers', after Michael Douglas's nemesis in the film *Fatal Attraction*[1], but actually being the victim of a vicious or stalking ex-partner is far from funny. Violence is more common than many people want to believe. Every year, some men and many more women are put in hospital, or the morgue, by brutal partners they wanted to leave or had left. Violence in a relationship may be one reason why the relationship breaks down. It's certainly a reason for many dissatisfied and unhappy people to stay in a relationship that has otherwise drawn to an end.

[1] Michael Douglas has an affair with Glenn Close but decides to end it. She can't accept it's over and stalks him, turning up at his home for a violent resolution during which she kills the family pet.

EMOTIONAL VIOLENCE

The threat in a relationship does not have to be open and
physical to be dangerous or damaging for those trapped in it.
Adults and children can be affected profoundly and permanently by emotional violence. Even if the menace is implied or
the intimidation is by humiliation or contempt, the resulting
fear or lack of confidence and esteem can be crippling. 'Sticks
and stones may break my bones but words can never hurt me'
is one of the more stupid sayings invented by someone who
had never been subjected to emotional bullying. Joanna, for
instance, can swear to the powerful effects of mere words.
She was married to Bob for fifteen years and they had three
children. When the children were fourteen, twelve and six
Joanna decided that she had finally had enough. The problem
was that she was terrified of Bob and felt utterly incapable of
coping on her own. She had been tentatively trying to raise
the matter with friends and family for some time. They could-
n't see a problem. Bob was a hard worker, they had a good
standard of living and he seemed fiercely proud and protective of his family. The only point of conflict they seemed to
have was over the fact that Joanna had insisted on sending
their eldest away to boarding school. It was one of the very
few things she had been able to stand up to Bob and
push through against his desires. What nobody realised, and
Joanna never said to any of the family including the child himself, was that she had done this to put him out of his father's
reach. The boy had had a bad stutter which Joanna was convinced was caused by her husband's bullying. While he never
hit any of the children, in private he humiliated and verbally
abused them. Joanna never had any bruises to show but she
felt permanently cowed by what he was capable of saying.
When she finally told her parents she intended to leave
they couldn't and wouldn't understand her. When she tried to

explain his behaviour, they wouldn't believe her. They suggested she see a psychiatrist and continued to insist that her husband was a loving partner and a perfect father and that she must be mentally ill to be imagining there was anything wrong with their marriage, or him. One day Joanna managed secretly to record Bob having a vicious go at the twelve year old. She sat her parents down and made them listen to every word. They were visibly shaken and from that point started listening to and supporting her. She moved the children in with them while she saw a solicitor about a divorce, getting an injunction to prevent Bob seeing her or the children except with a third party present.

IT'S NOT ONLY MEN

The stereotype of a violent partner may be a very different picture from the reality. We tend to assume it's only men who may put other people at risk and assume this only happens in certain social or economic groups. This is not the case. All sorts, shapes and sizes of people can put their partners and family in a state of anxiety and it can be women as well as men. Ray, for instance, was first hit by his partner Tara in the first year of their relationship. He was shocked speechless and only too willing to accept her explanation that she had lost her temper and that it would never happen again. When he finally left her twelve years later it wasn't until he sat down with a counsellor and went over what he had to recognise was a typical week that he could see how much he had come to accept destructive and extraordinary behaviour as normal. Ray routinely wore long-sleeved shirts, even at the height of summer, to hide the bruises on his arms. He never wore shorts because there were always scrapes on his shins. His colleagues jokingly referred to him as the 'man in black' because he almost always wore sunglasses to hide black eyes. His cat was regularly blamed for the scratches on his face. Ray had adjusted his behaviour to encompass Tara's and had become so used to her outbursts, and excuses for them, that he saw these as she pictured them; all his fault, deserved and thoroughly normal.

The most damaging aspect of violence in a relationship is that the lines become blurred between the person who does it and the person who has it done to them. The reasons why it happens can become increasingly confused, and responsibility for being hit can be passed from the hitter to the one being hit. From the outside it may seem obvious that if you are being hit you can refuse to put up with it and if the other person doesn't stop you should leave. But because violence often builds up gradually, the partner who is being hit or seeing it happen may find it creeps up on them. It may seem obvious that if your partner gives you a black eye, smashes your nose or breaks your arm you should walk out at once. But if the first occurrence was a push, the second a shove, the third a slap, it may be hard to find the point at which to ask for help or call a halt, until behaviour you might have objected to gradually becomes almost ordinary. But someone with a vicious partner may live with brutality even if it does arrive early on in the relationship and with extreme force. Sometimes, the person being hit stays in the relationship because they fear they or someone they love will be further harmed if they leave or try to leave. Sometimes, violence is forgiven because the perpetrator swears that it was a one-off, out of character event, that will never happen again. The excuse is accepted because the victim desperately wants to believe it was an aberration. More to the point, the partner who uses physical or verbal violence to get their own way or to show their feelings is more than likely to be skilled at making their victim blame themselves.

THE ONLY CURE

Using violence almost always goes hand in hand with a refusal to accept responsibility. The excuse, the explanation, may be 'You made me do it. It's your fault. If only you hadn't nagged me/contradicted me/made a mess/this wouldn't have happened. All that it will take for this never to happen again is for you to be different'. The difficulty, however, with dealing with violent partners and violent relationships is that the abuser's behaviour can never be changed by the person who is being abused. The more you try to fit in with the demands of the abuser, the more you strengthen the pattern. Any attempt to be quieter, more compliant, more devoted only confirms their belief that it was your fault in the first place. Violence has to do with the beliefs and feelings of the person who is dishing it out. The aim, and certainly the result, of violent behaviour is to damage drastically the confidence and the esteem of the abused and so allow the abuser to gain control of them and the situation. But for all the arrogance and apparent power of the abuser, the truth is that they do what they do because it is their own confidence and esteem that is at a startlingly low ebb. This is why they can never feel better just by having their victims ground down. The only cure for a violent relationship is for the abuser to deal with their own demons, not to visit them on other people. But since this requires the consent of, and hard work on the part of, the abuser it's not something that anyone else can do for them.

EMOTIONAL ILLITERACY

Violence can come about because the abuser simply doesn't have the words to express their anger or pain, and so uses their fists. It is often a result of emotional illiteracy, when the

words may be there but the person has never learnt or been
allowed to express feelings. This is one reason why men do
tend to be violent more often than women; women are often
brought up finding it easier to put their feelings into words,
while many men in our society are raised seeing emotions as
nasty, messy stuff best left to women. Violence is about power
and control. Violence is an out-of-control way of expressing
out-of-control feelings. It can, for instance, happen in relationships which are founded on unrecognised needs which change.
Tasha and James came for help because he hit her. They came
to realise that the trigger for James's violence was a change in
the script in their relationship. He was fifteen years older than
her and a teacher. Tasha's own father had died when she was
five and her mother didn't remarry until Tasha had left home
to go to college. What Tasha had always longed for was a
strong, capable man – a father figure – to care for her and protect her. James quite clearly wanted to be a carer and protector. What neither realised was that James's script originated in
a family in which violence was frequent. His own father was a
great believer in corporal punishment and thrashed him regularly. James had grown up terrified of this man, and trauma-
tised by the regular attacks. But rather than look back at his
beatings and admit to himself how scared, powerless and miserable they made him feel, James was drawn to a common coping technique. To get away and distance himself from those
terrible, scary feelings of powerlessness, James reframed the
situation as being one over which he had some measure of control. He told himself it never hurt, it was good for him and
character forming and that his father was right.

James needed to become the forceful man in charge of a
family in order to complete this rewriting, to shift himself out
of the victim category and into the pigeon-hole of authority
figure. To do so he had to take the place of the person who
victimised him, which is why he needed so badly to be that

Looking at Anger in Your Family of Origin

It can help you and your partner, and your family, if you can explore why violence has become a pattern in your relationship. Looking at anger and how it was expressed and shown in your own childhood may help all of you. This is often done best with a professional such as a counsellor, but you can get the ball rolling yourself by considering:

How was anger shown or not shown in your family when you were young?

Who showed the anger and to whom?

Was anyone not allowed to show anger? Who was that?

What was the effect of anger on (a) the person being angry (b) the person they were angry with?

What happened after the anger was shown?

How did the situation get back to normal?

Write down your answers and think about what it can tell you about the situation with you and your present family. Are there any similarities – any patterns that are repeating?

strong father figure. It may also be why he chose to become a teacher. While Tasha was happy to defer to him he felt secure about himself. He was authoritarian at home and strict with his pupils, but wasn't openly violent. But a few years into their relationship the balance of power changed. Tasha no longer needed a father, she wanted an equal partner because she wanted to be an adult partner herself. She wanted to change the balance of their relationship which James found difficult to look at doing. Any signs of her being able to stand on her own two feet triggered panic in James which led to his being violent. But finding an explanation for why violence happens is never a justification. In exploring the roots of his behaviour, James had the chance and the opportunity to understand and change what he did, not to excuse it.

A FORM OF ADDICTION

Abusive behaviour is difficult to change. In a sense, it's a form of addiction. Substance abuse and violent behaviour often go hand in had, one triggering the other. The reason is that the two often have a common root. Violence occurs because of emotional damage somewhere in the abuser's life. They resort to using their fists because they cannot cope with overwhelming and frightening feelings of anger, pain or loss, of feeling out of control and powerless. These feelings are threatening and frightening, so turning the violence outwards becomes a coping technique to exert some form of control. Substance abuse is a similar way of attempting to bring anxieties into line. When under the influence of drugs or alcohol, the user feels powerful, in charge and keeps their fears and lack of confidence at bay. Alcohol in particular is often a factor in a violent relationship but it may well be a mistake to think that if you simply banish the booze it will clear up the behaviour. It's more likely that both need to be tackled by understanding what is happening and why. The difficulty is that it is often very hard to offer help to someone stuck in either hitting out or abusing drink or drugs. However, there is an increasing awareness of violence in the family and more resources are available to help people who are being violent break the cycle. There is a growing number of groups and services for men who are violent, run by voluntary organisations or social services. You could ask your own doctor for advice on what is available in your area or contact one of the organisations listed at the end of this book.

CALLING A HALT

Whilst there is never any excuse for violence, there is a need to try to understand the causes of it in an individual. It can be very difficult to call a halt to the situation. It's tempting while in an abusive relationship to give it one more try or to feel there is no choice but to stay. Abused partners often remain because they cannot imagine being able to cope on their own – the abuse often leaves them so low in self-esteem and self-confidence that they believe the abuser when he or she says they are useless and incompetent. Often they stay because they fear for their own wellbeing or lives or those of their children if they attempt to go. Partners who have endured many years of threatening behaviour are often cut off from friends or family. The abusive partner may have deliberately driven other people away to isolate their victim. Or the abused may have done so themselves, out of misplaced loyalty or fear. Someone with a violent partner may feel that it would be impossible to shelter with friends or family, especially if they saw through or disliked the partner from the beginning or when violence became obvious. Someone whose self-esteem is already battered may find the thought of having to say 'You were right. It was a bad choice' the final straw. And there can be no doubt that leaving may be difficult. Threatened violence may spill over into the actual, while previous violence may escalate into worse. Someone who does resort to extreme behaviour can have a very fragile hold on reality. Violence often goes hand in hand with an all or nothing mentality which is what leads some partners to take the extreme position of saying and acting on the statement 'If I can't have you, no-one else will'. Victims also stay because they feel responsible – for the violence and for the violent person. Victims of violence often feel a terrible shame at what is happening in their family. Not only do they often accept the excuses that they asked for it, they feel guilty and embarrassed, as if being found to be the subject of violence is a reflection on them. But it's important to recognise that anyone being abused is NOT responsible for the abuse.

UNDERSTANDING ANGER

Anger becomes destructive and runs away with us when we don't understand why and when we feel it. Anger seldom comes out of the blue – it builds up. If you could recognise when you or someone you know feels rage, what makes it happen or get worse or what could be calming, you might be able to get it under control. Ask yourself these questions:

What makes you angry?
You may start by saying it's something another person does, but ask yourself how you *feel* at these moments. Is it their actions, or is it the way something in the situation triggers emotions – of helplessness, pain, fear? Can you remember feeling like that at any other time in your life? Could your anger

be about something in your past instead of what is going on now?

How would others recognise that you are angry?
Do you go pale or red, ball up your fists, go silent, get restless?

What are the first signs you notice in yourself?
Do you find yourself having difficulty in breathing or getting your words out? Do you feel panicky, frightened, confused?

What makes your anger increase?
Is there something you do yourself that makes it worse, or does being ignored or made the centre of attention drive you further into a rage?

What makes your anger decrease?
Would it help if people sat down and talked, or left you alone, to help you calm down?

What do you do with your angry feelings?
Do you shout, hit out, run away? Do you try to bury the feelings and pretend you're OK, go silent or keep on bringing it up? Do you pick fights with other people or shout at the family? Do you go and do the washing-up, go for a drink or a walk?

Write down your answers and look at them. Are there any clues in what you've written to ideas you could use to come up with a plan for how to deal with your anger, or that of someone in your family, next time? If you can understand why it happens, can you change the triggers that set off the anger? If you could see the warning signs, could you talk about it? If you know what makes it worse, or makes it better, could you decrease the first and increase the second? If you could find a helpful way of getting rid of the anger, could you make use of it?

EXPRESSING ANGER SAFELY

Anger is something all of us feel at some time or other. There is nothing wrong with anger, only with how we may express and show it. Anger needs to be recognised, accepted and expressed. You may fear the destructive nature of your anger for yourself and for those with whom you are angry. It may feel frightening and this may cause you to want to repress it. The problem with unexpressed anger is that it will come out, often in less helpful ways. Violence in the family tends to be about rage that isn't being handled in a constructive way. Sometimes that fury has its roots in the past, and is triggered by something that happens in the present and reminds the person of their earlier feelings of helplessness, loss or fear. It may become all the more violent because they are trying to keep the feelings and the anger under. Or it may show itself in subtler ways such as poor self-esteem, depression or ill health. This is why it is useful to have ways of expressing your anger safely. Here are some ideas – add your own:

Physical ways of expressing anger

- Throwing, kicking, punching soft objects such as pillows or soft toys.
- Ripping up newspapers or old phone books.
- Screaming loudly – do this somewhere deserted such as in the middle of a park or field or under a railway bridge when the train is going over or near a busy motorway.
- Shouting, jumping up and down or rolling around on a sofa or bed.
- Doing a work task with gusto – i.e. scrub a floor, dig the garden, polish windows and do it *furiously*.
- Doing some exercise – walk briskly, run, cycle, swim, go to a gym or keep-fit class.

- Throwing things at a target – throw stones at a post in the garden or soft toys at something indoors. Pretend the target is the person or thing you're angry with.

Non-physical ways of expressing anger

- Painting your feelings. Get lots of paper, lots of colours and lots of room and splash, slash and clash your emotions out in the open.
- Writing a letter. Put exactly what you are feeling down in words. Don't send it to the person with whom you are angry – the point of this is to dump it and get it out of yourself. When you are satisfied you've put it all down, burn it or rip it to shreds and let it go.
- Pretending the person you are angry with is sitting in front of you and tell them what you think of them.

When violence is an issue it may be useful to see it as a factor in itself. Violence doesn't happen because someone leaves the lid off the jam or doesn't laugh at a joke. Neither does it happen because love has waned and your relationship is in trouble. Anger may occur because of all or any of these but how you express that anger is something else. You may need therefore to make a separation in dealing on the one hand with the particular issues and on the other with the expression of them. In other words, you and your partner may want to discuss all the different excuses that are made by the person hitting out for losing their rag. But the first thing that has to be dealt with is the violent person's violence and the other person's fear. If you're the one being hit, the main point is that it is not your fault this happens. You can't stop or change the other person's behaviour – they have to do that for themselves. What you can do is stop being the victim. If your partner won't back off and let you feel safe, you do need to take steps to remove the threat from yourself and your family. That may be by getting away to a place of safety; it may be by getting professional help to remove and ban your partner from being near you and a threat to you.

Things to do to deal with domestic violence

Get out
Stopping the violence isn't your responsibility, just as it isn't your fault it started or continues. If your partner won't halt their violence to you or your family, go to a place of safety and negotiate an ending from there.

Say no
Sometimes, violence can be stopped by one person simply, calmly and forcefully calling a halt. People who hit out need you to be a victim. If you cease to be one, they can lose their power. Instead of reacting with your own anger or with fear, if you could hold up your hands in a gesture that says 'Stop!', you may find your attacker does so. But if this doesn't work, don't blame yourself or feel at fault. When you can, get yourself and your children to safety.

Put the responsibility where it belongs
Recognise that violence is *always* the responsibility of the person who hits. Don't accept their declaration or belief that anyone else asked for it, caused it, deserved it. Even if the row might have started elsewhere, it's the person who hits who chooses to do so, not the person who gets hit.

Don't accept bargains or blame
Don't accept promises that if you ignore it, just this once, it will never happen again, or if you agree to stay, the abuser will mend their ways, or that the assaults will stop if you change what you do. The violence happened because of them, not because of you.

Ask for help from your friends and family
Tell your friends and family what is happening and ask for

help. Forget your fears of being shown up or rejected – the violence isn't your fault and isn't anything *you* need to be ashamed of.

Ask for help from professionals
There are plenty of people who can help you, from your local police to Women's Aid. You can be given refuge, guided through the laws on injunctions, helped with counselling and mediation, advised on money. Just ask.

Don't necessarily close the door
Violent partners *can* be good parents. True, they may allow their brutality to spill over and affect their children after a separation, when they had left their children alone before; or they can take out their anger in verbal abuse, which can be every bit as damaging as hitting. But it may be more harmful to your kids to totally cut off all contact with a parent. Look to minimising risk by insisting on safe contact, with supervision at a neutral spot, before slamming the door altogether.

VIOLENCE AND ENDINGS

The threat of violence, emotional or physical, can complicate an ending. In relationships where you feel as if you are skating on thin ice both partners may often be struggling with the issues of low self-esteem. Someone who has been subjected to violence in a relationship or who senses it is a possibility may find it hard to stand up for themselves, or even to accept they have a right to do so. Violent partners sometimes consciously, more usually unconsciously, use their behaviour to subdue and dominate the people they live with. They use naked anger, humiliation or actual assault to cut people down to size, to make them feel unworthy and incapable and to do what they say. Violence rarely comes out of the blue even where someone may be shocked by a sudden outburst. Invariably, however, there is a slow and steady increase in physical or verbal violence which sets a tone.

But if you are living in fear, that's a reason to leave a relationship, not a reason to stay. You need to plan an escape and to access all the support that you can get. You also need to be very firm and very clear in expressing your fears. If you genuinely believe your partner is likely to harass or attack you, or has done so, look for help and get the back-up of the police and a solicitor. Above all, don't let anyone decry your fears. If you think you or your family are at risk, ask for help and don't give up until you have it.

Chapter Eight

SHARED PARENTING WHEN A RELATIONSHIP ENDS

When a family divides, you may face one of the most difficult and possibly most challenging tasks of your lives; how to manage shared parenting but divided lives. Many people assume the challenge to be whether you will stay in touch and how best to minimise your children's distress. One thing you may have to keep very firmly in mind is that, whilst being partners may have been a temporary state that, sadly, is now over, being a parent is permanent. You can be an absent parent, an irresponsible parent, an uncaring and unfeeling parent; once your children have been born however, the one thing you cannot be is not a parent. You may feel that not being in contact with your partner until Hell Freezes Over would be far too soon. As far as your children are concerned, losing the integrity of their family is the worse thing that has ever happened to them; losing touch with even a poor and sorry excuse for a parent would be one disaster too far.

OTHER PEOPLE'S FEELINGS

During, and in the aftermath of, a break-up it can be very hard to take other people's feelings on board, particularly if those feelings are very different to your own. Parents often make the mistake of assuming they know how their children feel and that this is in line with their own attitudes. It may be difficult to put yourself in their shoes, especially if you suspect you are not going to like what you'll hear. Young people often find themselves hiding their own feelings because they sense they are not welcome. It's one thing politely not to spoil somebody's birthday or a summer picnic because you don't want to confess that you are not feeling up to it. Having to pretend that you have nothing to say about the fact that your family has broken up is quite another matter. Children often become convinced that the break-up was their own fault because they can't ask questions or discuss their feelings about the events.

What makes family change so difficult for children and young people?

They feel powerless

Family change is never a young person's choice – kids aren't part of the decision to divorce, and kids seldom decide to walk away from their parents and their family. It's their parents who make these choices and these decisions and young people often feel utterly out of control and totally powerless in the face of your actions. So it's not just the decision, which they may not understand and may not agree with, that makes them feel so angry and upset; it's also the simple fact that it was something out of their hands. 'Bad behaviour' on children's part after a break-up may be because they're trying to get back a measure of power, or because they're showing, in the only way they can, how angry and hurt they feel.

They feel responsible

Young people feel responsible in two ways. They may get the idea that they caused or were a final, clinching, factor in the break-up – that if they'd been better children you might not have broken up. They can also feel that, now the split has happened, they are answerable for your happiness and wellbeing and so they have to behave in ways that please you. Children are often enormously sensitive to other people's feelings. They will often tell you what they think or know you want to hear because they fear that what they actually feel would hurt your feelings. Above all, they may be very aware that you are overwhelmed by your own anxieties. They'll work very hard not to burden you with theirs. If you are not aware of this it's very easy to take their declarations that they 'Don't care' and 'Can cope' and 'Just leave me alone' at face value.

They feel torn
Young people in a separated family feel tremendous divided loyalties. Whatever you feel about the other adult, and whatever either of you have done to your children in the break-up, kids love you both. They find it hard enough that the two people they love most are at war with each other. It only makes a difficult situation intolerable if you ask them to join in, too.

They feel ignored
Young people hate the fact that no-one asks them what they feel or think, or gives them any say in what is going to happen. Clearly it would be inappropriate to ask your children for their ideas on your arguments, or for permission to separate. But that doesn't mean you can't tell them what is happening in their family, and ask them how they feel about it. But when it comes to decisions that affect them – such as how you're going to organise living arrangements – there's no reason why they can't at least be brought into the discussion. Even very young children have opinions and certainly feelings you need to take on board.

DIFFERENT IDEAS

You and your children might have very different ideas about
how you are going to behave when a break-up has happened.
Whether the break-up was at your instigation or not and
whether you are relieved or upset at what has happened,
adults often respond by having a clear out and a change. You
may want to signal the end of the old and the start of the
new in some sort of dramatic way that both reassures and
energises you. Part of the ending of the relationship may be
that you move to a different house on your own with your
children and sometimes back into living with other family
members. And, of course, if another partnership is part of this
change there may be new people in your house or you may be
moving to new accommodation with them. The changes may
surprise and even delight you although some may depress and
frighten you. However they may seem to you, they are almost
certainly going to be alarming to your kids. It's bad enough to
lose your family and to have one parent move out. To have the
one who is remaining apparently alter personality is downright confusing. This is not to say that you should conceal or
deny the way you yourself are developing and the conse-
quence or significance of these changes to you. What it has to
mean, however, is that you need to discuss it.

Some changes, however, may have an even more drastic
effect and there may be dramatic differences in how they are
seen by parent and child. Some adults may want to go further
than simply re-inventing themselves and want to re-invent the
past. In your anger and disgust at what has happened to your
relationship it is very common for separating parents to want
to throw out belongings that show a shared history. It's common, for instance, for photographs to be thrown away, for
favourite clothing, CDs, books and belongings to go on the
rubbish heap because they remind a grieving parent of what

Names Matter

One aspect of the difference between adults and children when a relationship separates is the question of names. Women who have changed their names during a marriage or have taken their partner's name during a long-term relationship may be all too eager to re-name themselves. Taking a name is yet another ritual of transition. Women still tend to take the name of their partner when they marry, and then either revert to the name they had before the relationship or take on the one belonging to a new man in their life if there is one. Indeed, there are even increasing numbers of women who are taking on entirely different names. Some women take on family names or ones they simply choose, as a way of saying that while they don't want to be the person they were in the relationship, neither do they wish to go back to who they were before. The name they choose signifies a whole new beginning. And none of this is illegal or even needs legal intervention. You may go through the formal procedure of taking out a new name by deed poll but, in fact, it is just as effective and just as legal simply to take the new name and inform all the relative authorities that this is how you wish to be known in the future. Anyone can call themselves any name they like as long as this is not done with the intention of defrauding or deceiving.

Names aren't so much of an issue for men, who tend to keep the one they were born with for life. They are, however, an enormous source of conflict, confusion and pain for children. Just as with adults, children can choose to be known by whatever name they prefer. After a separation children tend to live primarily with their mother and she may go back to using her maiden name or take the name of a new partner. She may then want to change her children's names. This may be partly because it could be confusing for other people who may ask awkward questions that embarrass the children. But she may want to change their name to that of a new partner as a specific statement, making the point that she would like him to be considered as their new father. This may not be in the children's best interests. For that reason, if you alter your child's name yourself you may run foul of the law. If a man objects to his children losing his name he may apply to the courts and his wishes may be upheld. This will hold force until the children are old enough, when they reach their age of majority, to make their own choices. A compromise that some families adopt is for the children to take on a double-barrelled name that reflects the last names now used by both of their parents. So, Adam Smith, whose mother goes back to being Jane Jones, may call himself Adam Smith-Jones. And if all this seems unnecessarily complex and cumbersome you do have to consider the reason behind it all. Names are an identity and a way of displaying a tie. Women take on the names of their partners, or a couple creates a double-barrelled name, to show that they are a partnership and a unit. This is why when it breaks apart they may want to tell themselves, their ex-partner and the world at large how they feel through the discarding of that name. But for children the retaining of the link may be like a lifeline. Whether they manage to stay in touch with the missing parent or not they may want the name as a link to that part of their own identity and their origins.

has been lost. While this may remove what appears to be a sad part of your life from your attention, it destroys a child's entire history. Ten years of photographs may represent a quarter of your life, and a quarter you want to forget. It may be the whole of your child's life, and a part that they need to remember to know who they are and where they come from. But more important is the statement you make in wiping out the part of your life that brought them into being and the partner with whom you combined to do so. In getting rid of someone who was an addition to your life with whom you can do without – however unhappily or angrily – you start again and feel you heal a wound. In the eyes of your children, however, you are eradicating half of themselves. You are saying that what created them was a mistake. They can be forgiven for concluding that you wish they never existed either. At the very least what they have to face is the knowledge that there is a part of them that you hate. Destroying photos and other remnants of the past may seem to be creating a clean slate and may be inviting to adults. For the kids, it's destroying their memories, their foundations and their happiness.

CHILDREN AS BARGAINING CHIPS

After a break-up, children are often used as a trump card that can be withheld or bargained with by the parents. One parent may refuse to see their children, or threaten to stop the other one seeing them, unless the other agrees to their demands over money or other matters. Parents often play about with access, changing arrangements at short notice or 'forgetting', so a parent turns up to see their children and finds the family has gone out or have other family members there. Or children are used as messengers, sent with ultimatums or attacks when they visit the other parent. 'Mum says you have to get us new shoes', 'Dad says you're horrible'. Or they may be used as spies to gather ammunition and evidence. Children may find themselves being subjected to an interrogation when they get home, on everything from the money that was spent on them to who else was in the house with the other parent.

It's important to recognise what is going on here. By understanding what both of you are doing you may avoid getting drawn in to reacting emotionally. Money is often used as a way of buying love or controlling people, of showing value or withholding it. And children are often used as a form of coin, as something the other parent wants, needs and values and thus as a way you can get to them, to hurt or control them. The problem is that, unlike money, children have feelings of their own and using them hurts them. And the truth is that using anything – money, property, your kids – to make a point and affect your ex-partner actually doesn't work. The *only* way you can deal with unfinished business between you effectively is to do it, out in the open, upfront and honestly. Children who can't see a missing parent often grow up lacking in self-esteem and confidence and blame themselves. It doesn't matter who left or who's to blame – for their sake, contact needs to be made easy and arguments need to be kept out of it.

LOSING TOUCH

By the time two years have passed after the end of a relationship, half of all leaving partners – this is usually fathers – have lost contact with their children. The parent with full-time responsibility for the children may see this as a relief or a triumph. If the break-up was angry and upsetting, if there was continuing conflict, losing contact may at least bring what appears to be peace. If there was a new partner on the scene, the responsible parent may also feel that the other parent would only complicate matters. However, this is not the way children will see it. However confusing, however complex, however difficult, being in touch with both their parents may be, it is vitally important for children's wellbeing. This is the one glaring difference between your needs and your children's needs; you may need closure after a relationship ends while they need to continue their relationship with the person you no longer love. Continuing to co-parent while managing and acknowledging that your relationship is over is a real challenge, but it can be done.

SO HOW MIGHT YOU DO IT?

Shared parenting is hard work and can require complicated juggling. You need to remain in constant touch with your ex-partner, discussing with them all the details of your child's life – schooling, health, their friends, even consulting over haircuts and new clothes. Your children may live with the other parent as often and as much as they do with you – one week here and the other there, or weekdays with one, weekends the other. You may then split finances and contact with other people in your children's lives equally down the middle between you. Some parents have even experimented with living next door or in a split but partially shared home. But parents can share responsibility even when the bulk of time is spent with one parent. Children may live with one parent but talk with the other once, twice or more than three times a day on the phone or by e-mail or fax. This way, even children separated by many miles from a parent can feel that they are fully involved in their life. All this takes is the will and commitment to do it. The work is in setting up the systems to allow this and the co-operation of both parents. It is this co-operation, of course, that makes all the difference. It is very easy to allow your feelings for each other to spill over into your behaviour over your children. Effective shared parenting relies entirely on being able to separate these two, on being able to finish the argument, put it aside, and let it go and to forge a new friendship with your ex, to be, in other words, past lovers and partners and future co-parents. At the very least it means being able to put aside any remaining conflict for other times and other places so that when contact is about your children you can co-operate.

But you should also consider the concept of sharing, as being about more than parenting. Most of us in the situation of a split family see it as something we, as a parent, have to thrash out with the other parent, or on our own. You see your children as counters in the game or victims or problems. You may certainly feel you are protecting them and being a good parent if you do it all for them. Sadly, this may backfire in leaving them feeling even more powerless and pushed around. They didn't ask for you to go and separate – they now haven't asked for you to plan what happens with the rest of their lives. What may help all of you is to move towards seeing them as participants in the situation. They have their own rights, their own needs, their own opinions. They may also have their own suggestions and ideas. Even very young children appreciate being asked to chip in, with thoughts on how to deal with the circumstances. And the more they 'own' what you're all doing, the more in control they will feel.

When setting up your arrangements, consider these factors:

How will the children feel?
Ask yourself what messages the arrangements you want to make will send to your kids. If you want to make a totally fresh start, does this tell them that you want to wipe out everything from your relationship with their other parent, and how does this feel to them? Ask your children how they feel and talk it over with them. You may not be able to fit in with what

they would prefer you did, but at least you could reassure them about their fears and anxieties.

How will the children manage?

Running a separated life can be very confusing and hard work for your kids. If they are going to have two bases, they may need extra belongings – clothes, books, comforts – so they're never caught out at home or school, missing something vital. Or you may need to help them keep track of timetables so they keep on top of it. Asking kids to take responsibility for their own gear is all very well, but there are limits. Especially when 'forgetting' something and leaving it in the wrong home may actually be a way of telling you they want more time there, that they hate this to-ing and fro-ing. Consider, too, their own friends and social life. It may suit you very well to have them staying here one weekend, there another, but what happens when their friends in one location have an event or get-together, and you've sent them off to the other home?

How will you feel?

You are bound to feel divided and torn several ways by these arrangements. You may miss your kids terribly when they're with their other parent, and feel anxious and nervous. You may find yourself demanding your children come home or be in constant touch, saying it's for their sake. You have every right to feel jealous, angry, upset. You have no right to visit these feelings on your children, however. It may be important to recognise whether your anxieties about your ex or your children staying with them are about your own fears and when they may be realistic fears for them.

How will you manage?

In making arrangements for your kids, it is sensible to link them with your own needs, too. For instance, women often take on the day-to-day care of their children, having their kids live with them in the week and during school term, and sending them off to see Dad at weekends and holidays. This may seem practical but it isn't helpful. It means that mothers lose out on having free-time with their family, and never seem to have the opportunity to enjoy the off-periods with them. But it also means children only have special times with their dads. It means that only one parent has the chance to share real, everyday, ordinary family life with their children while the other takes the full burden of the work and the problems. In sharing the load, you also share the fun and in looking after your own interests, you may also help your kids.

---

8 Steps for Action

- Keep arrangements flexible and frequent.

- Ask the kids what they want and try to listen to them.

- Never, ever break an arrangement with a child. Reschedule dates or work around them, not the other way round.

- Schedule a weekly talk with your ex about your children.

- Make sure kids have space of their own – if not a room, a box or area that is theirs – in both homes.

- Let youngsters use the phone with no restrictions to keep in touch with the other parent. A mobile phone of their own gives them control of communication. So does an e-mail account they can access from any computer.

- Try to live near enough to each other so that your kids can make their own way – walking or cycling – between their two homes.

- If you're finding it hard, go to mediation.

COMING CLEAN

It may be very important to get support systems organised to help you and your children cope with these changes. We'll discuss family members in another chapter, but one of the most important places for young people, of course, is their school. Schools can be places of safety and security after a separation – or further torture. Studies show that schools that have clear goals about family change, and provide plenty of encouragement and support, become an important protective factor for children during a difficult time. A leading independent school head recently admitted that family breakdown causes more problems for pupils than drugs or any other difficulty. It may be useful to point out to your children's teachers that schools that do address the reality of their pupils' lives and offer relevant advice have fewer problems.

Schools need to know what is happening in your child's life. You may feel that keeping it quiet could protect them from the embarrassment or stigma of being from a broken home. Instead, you may let them in for far worse. When children lose one parent, they're often terrified the other may disappear too. They may start truanting or school refusing, staying at home because they think you might go, too, as soon as their backs are turned. Or their misery may turn to anger and lead to bullying, or depression so that they become the target of bullying. 'We didn't tell the school at once,' says Julie. 'We didn't want him marked out as having come from a broken, problem home. Then we found he was getting punished for fooling around, because they didn't know he had a lot on his plate. He was clowning around because he just felt so awful, it was a way of cheering himself up. And it also covered up from us the fact that he kept getting told off for forgetting his homework. He didn't tell the school the reason was he'd leave it with me or at his dad's and then be going to school from the wrong home.

And his father never came to any parent/teacher events because I kept forgetting to tell him and the school didn't know to send him information. I was so embarrassed when it all came out, until the head told me 30 per cent of the school was in the same position.'

Your children's school may be on top of this sort of situation and set up to give you the best possible help. You may, however, need to lobby for some awareness and action. Some schools need to be reminded that families come in all shapes and sizes and it's neither the shape nor the size that provides the best protection and care for children but the quality of what you have to offer.

THE SCHOOL AND YOU

You and your child's other parent may like to talk the following over with the school:

- Do teachers keep an eye on how children behave, out of as well as in their classes? If a child is disruptive, unhappy or failing at schoolwork, is family change seen as a factor?

- Is the 'culture' of the school welcoming, and accepting of family change? Find out if pictures around the school show families as other than two parents, two children.

- When teachers talk about home life, do they talk about 'carers' as well as about 'parents'?

- Do they recognise that children may stay in different homes for part of their week/month/year?

- Do teachers let children themselves define who they include as part of their family? It might be important to check out how the school asks pupils to describe their family. If they are expected to draw diagrams, are these as family forests or maps, which allow for all shapes and sizes of family, or as family trees which tend to expect one, static formation?

- Do they keep a record of your family circumstances, so teachers can be aware of arrangements? Are they aware of how living in more than one home may affect children's ability to do homework on time or arrive at school with the correct equipment? Do they list both (or all) family addresses, so parents with whom the child does not live can be contacted if necessary?

- Will they send invitations to parent/teacher meetings to more than one address?

- Are they clear who is responsible for and can make decisions about the child – it may be more than one person, it may be only one? When forms have to be signed or people contacted in an emergency, do they know who this should be and make sure it is the correct one? When homework diaries are signed, are they aware that this may be done by a variety of people?

- Are they happy to deal with different names without making the child involved feel singled out – children may have a name different to the one their parents use, and different to the one used by other children who share their home and are at the same school? How do they make sure the name used is one the child is happy about?

- How does the school decide which parent to discuss any changes with? Do they include other significant adults – new partners or relatives such as grandparents who may be closely involved with the children at this point?

- Does the school know of any organisations or services that may help, and how do they involve them or pass the information on to you?

PRACTISE WHAT TO SAY

It's your responsibility to tell your child's school, and other
people such as your doctor, what has happened. But it does
help them if you practise with your children what they might
tell anyone who asks, or when it is relevant. You could
rehearse with them an explanation such as 'My dad and mum
don't live together anymore. They still love me and they're still
my dad and mum, they just live in different homes. I see my
dad every week/I live with both of them, I'm at each home half
my week/I don't see my dad as much as I'd like but I know
he's still there for me'.

Shared Parenting

- Start from the principle that your children have two
  parents, and that they need and deserve to keep the
  connection with both of them.

- Other people may join your family or immediate circle
  and become important – step-parents, friends, professionals such as counsellors or teachers. They will be
  additional to, not replacing a parent. None of them can
  take the place of your child's two parents.

- Accepting the importance of two parents, ask yourself
  how you will make it easy for your child to maintain
  that link. You may need to finish the argument in one
  way or other, or to put your own anger and arguments
  on one side when it comes to dealing with the other
  parent and your child. You may need to set up a safe
  place to meet to discuss child-related matters.

- Encourage your children from an early age to feel able
  to talk to both of you when and how they please,

rather than expecting one of you to be the go-between for your children and the other parent. Encourage them to make their own arrangements and requests. Encourage them, too, to make their own complaints if they have a beef with the other parent – and with you!

- Don't undermine or complain about the other parent to your kids – what is wrong between you is your business and problem, not your kids. But neither should you protect the other parent from your child's anger or upset. If one of you has let a child down, you should know about it.

Chapter Nine
FAMILY MEMBERS

When a relationship comes to an end people often react by sinking into isolation and depression. We may long to unburden ourselves to people who care about us and seek their support. For many of us, however, this feels difficult or even impossible. Even if you have loving and supportive family and friends, you may have withdrawn from them as your relationship took a nose-dive, out of embarrassment or shame. You may have lost touch, overwhelmed by your problems or simply having too much on your plate to maintain the link. They may not have been as caring and protective as you might have wanted, so you may not see them as people to go to for help. Sometimes they might have been critical of your relationship and your partner. Perhaps their motives might have been loving but you may have experienced it as criticism and pulled away from them. Now it's all gone wrong you might feel that they would crow and say that they had told you so, or just be embarrassed and not know what to say. Even if they hold their tongues you may feel too ashamed or mortified to want to reveal yourself to them. Or it simply may be that you feel so battered and bruised that your first instincts are just to retreat into a deep hole and pull a blanket over your head.

WE ALL NEED SUPPORT

Whatever your reasons, if your instincts are to try and face the ending of your relationship on your own, fight them. We all need support systems and it's absolutely vital for us to retain or re-forge links with friends and family in the wake of a lost partnership. When a relationship ends we often feel totally compromised. Whatever actually occurred, we may well feel in some way to blame. If we hadn't said that, if we hadn't done this, if somehow we had been nicer, sexier, more attractive people, this would never have happened. Whatever was said or done in your relationship and during its ending, everyone involved is likely to emerge with their self-esteem and self-confidence reduced. This may be the reason that you shy away from contacting or leaning on friends or family. In fact, it's the main argument for your being and keeping in touch with them. Put aside for the moment any reservations you have about how they behave and consider what family and friends could, at their best, do for you. On the practical side they can help with advice, help and – if you have children – childcare when you need it. On the emotional side they can restore your self-esteem by showing you that they still love and care for you. The unconditional love family and friends can give may reassure you that you really are still loveable, valued and cared for, in spite of what has happened.

For those of us who are lucky it may be fairly obvious that the people you would fall back on at a time like this are your own. You would hope that your own relatives and people who have been your friends before or during your relationship would stand by you. But you may have doubts about the people who don't have an obvious link to you – your ex's relatives, people who might have thought themselves more your partner's friend than yours and, indeed, some mutual friends. You might feel inclined to cut your losses on all of these. But it's worth considering before making assumptions that cutting ties with one person necessarily means cutting all the ties you might have made with them or through them. You and your children may need all the support you can get, so don't turn your back on anyone if you can help it.

If you have children, this is especially important. Keep in mind the fact that while your tie to your ex-partner was a question of choice that was made and can be unmade, your children cannot say the same. Their connection was not simply by marriage or proximity, it was and is through their genes or their upbringing. Your in-laws are simply people that you have a legal bond with through your partner. Once that bond was dissolved your link to them, both legally and possibly emotionally, can be said to have melted away. But your children remain connected and may quite desperately want to retain both the sense of connection and actual contact.

GRANDPARENTS

Grandparents are terribly important for kids, and when a family breaks up they are often the only point of stability. Your mum may change her name, your father may no longer be living with you and you could suddenly find yourself with a step-parent, step-siblings and eventually half-brothers and sisters. With all the movement and confusion, the one thing that may remain are your grandparents, whose relationship to you never alters. Sadly, grandparenting is a role lost in many families, even where there hasn't been a divorce. At it's best, the relationship between a child and a gran, nan or gramps can be a tremendous boost to a kid's self-esteem and confidence. And a grandparent's home can remain as the one place that a child can go to for sanctuary, knowing that amongst all the upheaval, this place will be the same as it has ever been. Grandparents can offer more than just a place for kids to retreat to for a break, allowing you to recoup. They can also afford a perfect, neutral meeting point where kids can be passed from one parent to another, or ex-partners can meet to discuss their shared child-care tasks.

RETAINING LINKS

It's important to retain links with the parents of your co-parent too, not just your own, even when contact with your ex-partner breaks down. Some grandparents take sides, nastily, but often they can be more objective than their own children. They can provide an unconditional love and welcome for their grandchildren at a time when much of the love they are grasping at appears to be conditional, on their being 'good' or 'loyal'. While a child's dad or mum may look at them and see the other parent they are angry with, the grandparent may still be able to offer the love of a relative without seeing a taint. They also have time, when parents are taken up with the demands of arrangements or emotions and have little to spare. The same can be said of other relatives, sometimes. Uncles and aunts and cousins from both sides of the family may be able to show your children that even if their nuclear family of mum and dad is coming apart at the seams, there is still the wider family to stand firm and be around them.

This consolation may be helpful for you, too. Mother-in-law jokes aside many people find a closeness with their in-laws that they would like to retain even when the relationship with their son or daughter has ceased. And it's not just the partner's parents. Your ex brothers- or sisters-in-laws, your uncle- or aunts-in-law and even cousins you've acquired through your relationship may have filled something in your life which you would hate to let go. The sad truth is, however, that family often interprets their place in a split up as being on one side of a barrier, at either end of a battlefield. The presumption is that sides are drawn up and that you are supposed and expected to back up your own family member. You ex-partner's family may feel that they would be showing disloyalty if they were to continue being in touch. While grandparents may continue to be in touch with their grandchildren, however close and loving they may continue to be with the kids themselves, they may be stilted and awkward with the other parent. When it comes to family gatherings the assumption may be that while the children are welcome the adult is not. Expecting that sides have to be taken can be particularly difficult when there is bitter conflict as a part of the break-up. There may be intense bitterness on the part of the partner who feels they have been badly wronged if their partner's family continue to back them up come what may. Of course, families don't always split along blood lines. One partner may find their own relatives taking the other person's side if everyone has decided that it was their behaviour that was to blame for the split. It can be bad enough if at the centre of all this you have just two adults dissolving their relationship. It's obviously far worse when there are children caught in the crossfire.

So much is lost when a relationship breaks up. You don't only lose your partner, you lose a sense of stability, that understanding that certain things can be trusted and will remain. This is frightening and depressing for adults but can be possibly terrifying for children. So while the walls of your own small unit are fading it's that much more important to ensure that you retain other networks. However hard it may seem it may be vital for you to take the initiative in keeping these going. If it's possible this is something that you and the partner from whom you are separating should do in concert. It becomes that much easier for other people to put aside anger, bitterness and not take sides if they see that you are together on this. Even if you are still in a high state of conflict it's still possible for you to appeal for support and to set the tone for it to be non-confrontational.

FIRST MOVES

As soon as a decision has been made, get in touch with friends and family and lay the situation in front of them. Tell them you are separating but that however sad and upset you may feel about it, and whatever feelings they may have about it, you would very much like contact with them and their support. Stress that you don't want this support to be a matter of taking sides but that you would understand if they found this difficult. If there are children involved underline the fact that both of you remain committed to them and to being parents. Even if they may find it hard to face you would they please put aside any embarrassment or anger when it comes to seeing your children. When you do see members of your own family hold firmly to the line of not allowing criticism of a child's other parent. It may feel entirely satisfying to hear your friends and family tell you what a total loser and waste of time the other person may be and how you are well rid of them. If this is done at any time and in any situation where children could possibly hear – and that means within five miles of them – it can be horribly destructive. And if you continue to dwell on your ex-partner's shortcomings you won't help yourself to move on. Don't forget that laying the blame on the other person and being entirely critical of them can often backfire. The more your family stresses how terrible this other person was and how much they always knew it would come to a bad end the more they undermine you. It doesn't help you to trust yourself – your ability to chose a partner, your ability to manage a relationship – to be told that you've chosen a total loser. It also doesn't give you hope for the future. If you've made such a hash of it this time you may be convinced you wouldn't be able to make a better one next. And indeed families may well want to offer a certain type of support and help for exactly these negative reasons. They may get some satisfaction from you having come running back to the fold. They may be bolstering up their own self-esteem by seeing yours ground down.

NEGOTIATING HELP

The way forward then is to negotiate for help, support and contact adult to adult. You can ask for a shoulder to cry on and arms to hold you while still making it clear that you are a grown-up who intends to move on and remain in adult mode. You can also be fairly firm about what sort of help you want, in what sort of manner. You are not being ungracious or mean if you put your foot down about not wanting advice that leads to conflict or bitterness.

When Linda, for instance, broke up with her husband, her best friend was abusive and angry about him. 'She told me she'd never liked him, that he was a bastard and the best thing I could do was take him for every penny he owned and make sure he never saw the kids, ever again. Well, I was upset with him but this wasn't what I needed to hear. Our daughter adored him and he'd always been a good dad, whatever he did to me. The problem was that this friend just about made an ultimatum – if I didn't take her advice, she'd never speak to me again. I cried for days and really had sleepless nights over it. The last thing I wanted was to lose her, but I know what she was saying was wrong for us. I ended up telling her that it really hurt, what she was doing, but the bottom line was that however bad he'd been to me, I couldn't stop my Lianne seeing her dad, and wouldn't want to. And because I didn't make a fight of it, he behaved pretty well about money and every-thing. Things were a bit iffy with my friend and me for a time, but she ended up coming round and apologising. We're still friends, I'm glad to say.'

HELP OR HINDRANCE?

We all want friends and family to be on our side, and help us out. It may be hard for them, and us, to see how this is best done. Even people who love you can sometimes give advice, and act in ways, that sabotage our best efforts. The problem is that if they are our family, or our friends, we sometimes feel that we have to accept what they offer on their terms. Even when they're telling us to cut off contact with an ex-partner, when we can see negotiation would be better, we feel torn between doing what we think is best and pleasing the people on 'our side'. What you may need to do is be quite ruthless in working out what is best for your immediate family and you. You may need to divide all your contacts into those that help, and those that hinder your life at present. Spend time with the first group and tell the others that you love them, but will 'take a rain check' on seeing them for the time being, thank you very much. It isn't being selfish, unkind or unreasonable to limit your time with the people who make life hard for you and increase it with the ones who are making life easy for you.

Make a list of family and friends, such as the one below:

Your mother
Your father
Your sister/s
Your brother/s
Your ex-partner's mother
Your ex-partner's father
Your ex-partner's sister/s
Your ex-partner's brother/s
Your friends
Your ex-partner's friends
Your work colleagues

By the name, fill in whether you feel this person helps or hinders you in managing and feeling good about yourself and your family at the moment. When you see, in black and white, who is on your side and who is not, you may be able to make choices.

OTHER HELP

If your friends and family don't come through for you, don't despair. It's neither your fault nor because of any failure or behaviour on your part. The reason they draw away is probably because of their own difficulty in coming to terms with what is happening to you, and how they identify with that in their own lives. In other words, it's their problems that make them take a step back, their problem that they can't help and their loss that you will go elsewhere. Take the opportunity to make new friends and contacts who can help you deal with it. Look around for other people in the same situation – there are plenty. You could find them in groups such as the National Council for the Divorced and Separated, One Parent Families or Gingerbread. Your local library is the place to find out about local self-help groups, social clubs and activities.

Chapter Ten

LIFE AFTER SEPARATION

The initial impulse when you realise your relationship is coming, or has come, to an end may be to deny it. You may find yourself fighting hard to keep it going, to revitalise it, and fighting even harder to deny to yourself and everyone else that there is a problem. There comes a point when using your energy in this way really is flogging a dead horse. However good it might have been, however good you may believe it still had the potential to be, you need to let go and move on. The fact is that no single person and no single relationship is ever The Only One. There really is life after separation and it's time for you to discover that fact.

COPING WITH CHANGE AND LOSS

How we cope with the ending of one relationship and move on to a new life often depends on a variety of aspects. Whether we have helpful friends and family, whether we have a good opinion of ourselves, can have quite an effect on how we weather the change. Three features make it more likely that you fare well when a relationship ends.

1. *What else is happening*

Loss is made far worse if other major life changes come along at the same time. You are likely to find it easier to cope if:

- You (and your children, if you have them) can stay in your home.
- You have a job or are in education, and can continue as before.
- Your income stays much the same.
- You stay in contact with people, places or pets you value.

2. *The sort of person you are*

Your ability to cope with grief and loss changes at particular times in your life, and some people have more resilience. You are likely to weather a loss better if:

- You have self-confidence and value yourself.
- You feel in charge of your life, not at the mercy of fate or luck.
- You are in good health.
- You are prepared to talk about your feelings.

3. *Support networks*

Whether you cope with loss often depends on the presence of family and friends, your willingness to use the help they might offer, and their ability to offer the help you need. You are more likely to cope if:

- Someone is there for you when you need them.
- Your friends and family can listen and allow you to cry without trying to belittle your grief.
- Your friends and family can put their own feelings, opinions and needs aside while listening to you.

You can use this as a plan of action. Ask yourself how you fare on each item. For each area you can tick as a 'Yes', identify it as an area of strength. You can focus on this as something you can rely on. For each area you shake your head at and cross as a 'No', see it as a challenge that needs working on. This isn't a failure, it's a reminder of something you can improve and enhance, and that you will do.

BARRIERS TO SURVIVAL

The main barrier to surviving on your own after a separation, whether or not you have kids, is usually your own lack of belief in yourself. Whether you chose to make the break or the break was forced upon you, most of us after a relationship ends feel lacking in confidence and self-esteem. We feel that we have failed and as well as guilt we experience enormous fears over whether we are capable of coping on our own. We also often have fears about making and maintaining any other relationship. After all, we may tell ourselves, if we couldn't do it last time we won't be able to do it next time either. Making new relationships, on the foundation of a past relationship and its break down, isn't easy.

Starting again after some period of being in a settled relationship has quite a few hazards. You may be so used to being half of a couple that you can't think of yourself as an independent person, with rights and desires of your own. You may, indeed, have never been on your own, having gone straight from being a student, living at home or in some sort of sheltered housing, to being with someone. You may find it hard to manage on your own, being unused to dealing with money, budgets or other day-to-day details. You may find the thought of being alone hard to bear. To their own surprise, many newly-single-again people find being on their own can be one of the advantages of separation. You can eat crackers in bed at midnight with no-one to complain. You can pursue that hobby you really liked, with no-one to laugh at you or demand your time and attention. You can manage, with no-one to drag at your self-confidence. A period of standing on your own two feet with no-one by your side may do wonders for your self-esteem and allow you to get your life, and yourself, into perspective.

If you do go looking for a new partner, however, you may come up against some particular difficulties, following a separation. On the purely practical level there is the difficulty of meeting new people. When you are in your teens and twenties most of the people of your age will be single like you and it is not difficult to find partners. Not only will you be socialising in places where you are all looking for the same thing, but the likelihood is that where you learn, where you work and where you go in your leisure hours are all conducive to finding and dating and linking up with romantic partners. Coming back onto the market a few years later you will find it has all changed. The assumption is that most people your age will already be in relationships. Working patterns may have changed so that most of the people you are with – if indeed you work somewhere where there are plenty of other people – will already have partners. And there is also no doubt that, unlike twenty and even unlike ten years ago, the workplace is no longer seen as somewhere where you are supposed to be flirting and dating.

'THE MOVES'

But the main difficulty for someone seeking a partner after a break is the fact that you may have forgotten 'the moves'. There is a definite skill in meeting and greeting. You have to go through certain hoops in making yourself available, making it clear that you are interested and in taking the risks of lowering your emotional defensive barriers. You have to recognise that you need to get to know people and be adept at carrying on the 'small talk' conversations that both reveal and discover. You have to be prepared for the hard work of learning about another person and allowing them to learn about you, which all may seem clumsy, time consuming and disappointing when you've been in a settled relationship. It's a lot easier when you know someone. You know how they feel, you know what they are going to do and there is a certain shorthand you build up between each other. One of the reasons you may retire in frustration, annoyance and disappointment from a new relationship is the conviction that another person can't possibly love and understand you or give you what you need as well as your last partner. The truth is that your old partner didn't necessarily have anything unique nor is the new one necessarily lacking. What you are missing is that the new one won't yet have the advantage that the old one had of months if not years of acquaintance.

What is unique about new relationships is the knowledge that you've been here before and it failed. There is often a sense of failure, of incompetence, a lack of trust, of being doomed. Both you and any new partner may feel you are operating in the shadow of someone else and that there is an invisible rival. A new partnership may suffer from a feeling of competitiveness, that it has to be better than the last one and that comparisons are always being made. This is, of course, why we are often driven to try to cut out and wipe out not just evidence of a past relationship but even our own acceptance and acknowledgement that someone else had been there. We seem to feel that love can only be true love if it is first love so that we try to reassure ourselves and everyone else that yes, this is the first time we have really been in love and no, anything else was simply a mistake. Such a painful denial of your past is both difficult and hurtful enough when there is only you to consider. It has especial difficulties if you have children.

STATISTICS ON YOUR SIDE

Having children underlines that someone was there first. It makes it far harder to persuade yourself and your partner that you have been waiting, Sleeping Beauty-like, for them to come along, and it also make it far more painful to yourself and your family if you make the mistake of trying to do so. What is unique about families of divorce and separation is that they are born out of loss and often have very confusing and confused attachments within them. One of the good pieces of news about life after separation is that on present statistics over 50 per cent of divorcees remarry. As divorce and separation become not just common but the norm this will increase. In fact, by 2010 it is predicted that most people will, throughout their lives, have a series of long-term relationships rather than expecting to have only one. You may well link up with someone and create a home with them. You may marry and you may have children. You are highly likely then to split up and go on and do the same thing with someone else and possibly to do this several times. So the figure of 50 per cent of divorcees remarrying or forming new settled partnerships is most likely to climb to almost 100 per cent. This isn't always good news, of course, for those within those relationships. At the moment, at least 50 per cent of remarriages end in divorce, a quarter of them breaking down in the first year. The likelihood is that the enormous difficulties of managing not only a new relationship built upon one that collapsed, but a new family containing children with divided parents makes this a difficult task. The challenge that faces you in your life after separation is how to make it work – because work it can.

You can kick your new life off to a good start by reviewing what you expect from yourself, your life and any relationships you may have in the future. You may expect too much from yourself, too little from everyone else. If you're not getting or giving what you expect, you might be feeling let down, cheated or inadequate. And if you expect too little, you may actually stop people or situations coming good for you because you force them to live down to your expectations. There's no point in trying to change your life if what may actually be at fault is your expectations.

Expectations

Sit down with a pad of paper and a pen/pencil. Ask yourself:

* What do I expect from myself?
* What do I expect from life?
* What do I expect from a relationship?

The sorts of ideas you might find yourself putting down could be:

What do I expect from myself?
* I should always be competent, strong, in control
* I should have a partner, or be shown up as a failure
* I should know how to meet new people
* I always fail at relationships
* I'm a terrible parent
* I should keep a perfect home

What do I expect from life?
* Life would be fair
* People always let me down
* My family should love me, no matter what

What do I expect from a relationship?
* I'd be safe and loved
* I'd always have someone to care for me
* I wouldn't need any other people
* It will last for ever
* It will never change

When you've added your own ideas, think them over. Are your expectations realistic? Where did you learn to expect these things? Are they helping or hindering you in moving on?

Moving on

PUTTING A POSITIVE SPIN

The most important and effective strategy for living life after separation to the full is to put a positive spin on it. There are many elements that make your life after a separation different from that before. But for every drawback you may come up with there is an advantage. You may feel rejected and a failure for having had your relationship disintegrate. What you need to do is put Gloria Gaynor[1] on the sound system and tell yourself that you will survive. This isn't a *failure*, it's a *transition*. Finding that one relationship no longer fits is a prelude to others. It's not that you couldn't make it work, it's that in common with the majority of people you have found that society and relationships are moving on. This means that you aren't 'on the shelf', you are 'mature and experienced'. You aren't 'abandoned' or 'left behind', you are 'ready for something new'. Sit down and write out all the negative statements that occur to you which you have being saying, or have heard said, about your state, your situation and your life after separation. Then rewrite every single one with a positive slant. Do it with a friend or family and you may find yourself in fits of giggles at the ridiculousness of it all. But you could discover that depression and despair are really a result of looking at things in a downbeat way. You could start feeling more positive if you approach it differently.

Putting a positive spin on the way you see your separation and life after separation is also a way of coming up with a plan of action. Your list of all the problems and drawbacks of your life will show you where you may want to make changes. If, for instance, you put down the fact that you feel lonely, unsupported and that making ends meet is a problem, or that having full responsibility for childcare is a burden, you can

---

[1] Gloria Gaynor, disco diva, is the woman who sings that anthem for all women facing an ending, 'I will survive'!

see the areas which you will want to change. You may feel isolated and alone. You no longer have the partner you had and that may cause you to feel as if no-one cares, no-one understands and there is no-one who can back you up. This simply isn't true. Whether you want to talk to someone who understands or get help with practical matters such as training, job opportunities, financial advice or meeting new people, there will be people and an organisation that can help you. What is needed is for you to take the first step in deciding what you need, picking the ones that can be of help and then approaching them. You have to do the work in taking the actions that they might suggest but they will have done much of the slog for you by at least researching and having at their fingertips the advice you need.

PARTICULAR COMPLEXITIES

There are, of course, particular complexities in life after separation when you have children. On one level pulling yourself up, being strong and coping with a life on your own can sometimes be easier. You may allow yourself to collapse in a sodden puddle and wail that you can't possibly manage on your own when there is only you and the cat to look after. But even though you feel robbed of willpower and incapable of dealing with the big bad world on your own, when you have kids you are forced into a more adult mode. You may be all at sea with finances, confused with areas you've never had to cope with before but you are slightly more likely to get on and do it if you need to look after, and keep up a front before your kids. The drawback, of course, of managing this new state of your life when you have children is that you have to deal with their emotions and behaviour as well. Even if you get over your own nervousness about making a new relationship and pick your way through the minefield of how you and they feel about this not being a first love, both you and any new partner have to negotiate a new relationship with due consideration to your kids.

There is a very delicate balance to be established in introducing new partners to children. It's highly confusing for them if they keep meeting people who only last a week or a few months. Young children in particular tend to assume any new partner may be there for life which puts tremendous strains on a new budding relationship but also puts them into a constant turmoil. They may desperately like the idea of a new dad or mum and feel constantly let down, or they may totally hate the idea and so live in a permanent state of apprehension and anger. But neither does it help for them to be kept in the dark and suddenly presented with someone. They may then feel resentful and bitter that you've been carrying on behind their backs and deceiving them.

DIFFERENT FEELINGS

Just as your children would have had different feelings to you about a separation – you may have wanted it, they would not – you may have a very different approach to them in handling life after the event. Your wellbeing may depend on seeing the past as finished and closed, a part of your life that is now over. For your own emotional health you should recognise how much it meant to you and keep in touch with those bits in you that are a result of it, but you may not want or need to keep in touch with a past partner. You need to look forward in order to move on. In contrast, your children very much need to keep one foot in the other camp. Not only do they need to see reminders of your former partner and life with them, in the shape of pictures or belongings that recall the shared times, they need to talk them over and keep them alive. Their feelings and needs require that link, and it may mean that their fantasies are of a reconciliation. Against all the odds and all the evidence, young people will believe for a long time that their parents might, one day, reunite and make them a 'proper' family once again. New partners, of course, throw a real spanner in the works, which is why young people may be so hostile to them, or even the idea of them. Trying to get a child to be reconciled to the idea of a new person in your life, especially by trying to get them to like this interloper, misses the point. Your new love may be fantastic, wonderful and better in every way than their dad or mum. They aren't, however, their dad or mum and he or she is the person they want back in their lives. In fact, liking a new adult may be the very thing that sets them off into depression, anger and 'bad' behaviour. It may feel bad enough that you betray the memory of their missing parent by falling for someone else. It's far worse if they come under the spell and are disloyal by accepting them too. Kids can also be scared that a new partner for you means they might be heading for trouble. If you've survived the end of an old partnership and moved on to a new one, might you next decide to get rid of them too, and move on to new kids, new family?

FAMILY RITUALS

This is why attitudes, values and family rituals can become battlegrounds in new families. Family festivals can be a time when children think about a missing parent, and feel loss and pain. Seeing a new person in a parent's place can be the trigger for upset, and enjoying the occasion can be the cause of guilt and self-blame. Young people may then act up at the very times you think they should be happy, or feel you have gone out of your way to please them, and it may get fraught and miserable.

Young people may also pick attitudes and values as a battleground on which to show their objections to your new life. What they are really objecting to is the change in their life that has come about with your separation. What they may choose to shout about could be new ways of doing things in your family – discipline, schedules, arrangements and belief systems. All young people show their independence at some time by saying 'no', and teenagers display rebellion to their parents by having apparently different beliefs and moral codes to the 'old fogies'. Children in separated families can object to their situation by being more rebellious, more bitter, at an earlier age and for longer, than their peers in original two-parent families. They have more to object to, so do it louder.

FITS AND STARTS

It's helpful to remind yourself of two things when looking at your new life after separation. One is that you don't go from one life to another in a one quick leap, nor do you adjust overnight. You'll have a series of fits and starts, of advances and retreats. How you manage and how you see it will waver from old perspectives and old habits, to new ones, from being upbeat to being in despair. This is nothing to worry about and exactly as you should expect. The second is that your feelings and ability to manage will constantly come up against new challenges. We tend to feel that life proceeds on a level; once you're unhappy, you stay unhappy and once you're content, you stay so. We feel that if we have trouble during a 'normal' experience in life such having a baby, getting married, our kids becoming teenagers, it's because we don't know what we're doing, or our kids are problem children. The truth is that all these and many more are what we call common 'crunch points'. 'Crunch points' are those times in your life when you're up against decisions, feelings, changes, in you or in your family, that are troublesome and involved. They're transitions – bridges from one time of life to another. Having a new baby, experiencing your kids going through the teenage years, being responsible for family obligations, marriages and weddings, and death, can all be 'crunch points'. Every single one of them is difficult to deal with and every single one of us finds it hard to cope with them. So you're actually being perfectly normal in having a hard time. Knowing you're not unusual and having advanced warning that these will be tricky situations, tricky times, can help.

10 Things to Help Your Kids Move On

- Allow them the chance to voice negative feelings and fears.

- Schedule special time with each of your children – do something with them you know they really like.

- Get in the habit of telling your kids how much you love and value them, just for being them.

- Talk to them about your having social and romantic relationships in future. Reassure them that a new partner for you doesn't mean your relationship to them changes at all, not does it change their relationship to their other parent.

- However badly they may behave, understand it's bad behaviour, they aren't bad kids. Accept their mixed feelings about the changes in their life and help them talk it through.

- Encourage them to keep and display pictures, and talk over events, of the past.

- Encourage them to see family members such as grand-parents, aunts, uncles and cousins.

- Talk to them about festivals and family events. What would make them sad, what would make them happy about these? Can you create new traditions, keeping elements that please you all and help them feel a positive link to the past is maintained, while providing a bridge to the future?

- Help them to rehearse telling other people about their family.

- Whether you are moving home, adjusting to your partner no longer being there or having new people move in, plan a change around with your kids. You need to balance their need for security and sameness with a fresh start and a step forward. Ask their thoughts on a rearrangement of furniture, decorating or an 'All Change' in who has what room.

20 Things to Help You to Move On

- Remember one good thing you shared with your ex.

- Think of one good thing about your new life.

- Tidy your home, throwing away things you really won't need but putting the things you want to keep in order.

- Move the furniture around – celebrate a new beginning with a different arrangement.

- Go through your wardrobe. Divide everything into three piles – stuff you wear all the time, stuff you've worn in the last year, stuff you haven't worn for a year. Give the last to a charity shop, review the second again, and have a long look at the first.

- Have a make-over. New hair cut, new grooming and new

styles. Then look at your clothes again and see if you can get rid of old fashions, award yourself some new.

- Go for a walk, a run, a cycle or try an exercise class. Make a date to do that at least twice a week from now on.

- Set your alarm clock and get up to watch the sun rise.

- Visit your local leisure centre or college and book a class – learn salsa, car maintenance, skiing, French.

- Think of something that scares the pants off you – and go and do it.

- Pick something you always think of as a special treat – a bottle of champagne, a new CD, a massage. Buy it for yourself and enjoy – you deserve it.

- Call/see/e-mail a friend and have a chat and a laugh. Discuss only happy things – no moaning, bitching or complaining.

- Make one new contact today – say Hello, smile and chat to someone.

- Let your imagination run riot in planning a holiday away – the holiday of your dreams, if you win the Lottery.

- Work out what made your dream holiday so special and use those elements to plan a break you could manage.

- Do something that has a result that satisfies you – do the gardening, cook a special meal, decorate the bathroom. Bask in your achievement.

- If you have a cat or dog, give it an hour of your time. Play with string, throw a stick or go walkies.

- Put something living in your living room – a bunch of flowers, a pot-plant.

- Turn the TV, radio or stereo up loud and dance.

- Buy a present or arrange a treat for a friend or family member.

A FINAL WORD

Whether a new relationship is part of it or not, your new life is a new beginning. The end of something may be how you see it at first – a parting, a loss, a source of pain and sadness. But however difficult this may be at first, you can rise to the challenge and make it a positive advance. Every change in life involves a sort-of death. When you became a child, you lost the joys of being a toddler. When you became an adult, you lost the heady delights as well as the ghastly anguish of being a teenager. When you got married, you stopped being a single person, with all the joys and advantages as well as all the drawbacks of that. But this change involves a sort-of birth, as well. Life is a passage, a procession of states and each and every one of them has some drawbacks, some advantages; some bliss and some misery. You can reconcile the ending of the old life with the beginning of a new one, by recognising that this isn't a source of shame or guilt. You can feel apprehensive and nervous, but see this as the fear anyone would feel when on the brink of something new. The trick is recognising that your anxieties are normal, your situation is normal, and that you can cope. You're embarking on an altered situation, and while it may be different to your previous one, that doesn't mean it will be any the worse. You may need help, you will certainly want advice and support; but you can manage your new life, and you will.

USEFUL ADDRESSES

There are many professional or self-help organisations and agencies that you can call on for help before, during or after a separation:

Counselling and mediation

Relate can help with any relationship worries. As the largest relationship counselling organisation for individuals and couples, Relate helps thousands of people who are single and separated, married or divorced to manage their relationships. Their young people's service (eleven to eighteen) and Psychosexual Therapy Service are very popular too. You'll find the address and phone number of your local centre in your phone book. Or contact headquarters at:

Relate
Herbert Gray College
Little Church Street
Rugby
Warwickshire CV21 3AP
Tel: 01788 573 241
Website: www.relate.org.uk

In Scotland, contact **Couple Counselling Scotland**
40 North Castle Street
Edinburgh EH2 3BN
Tel: 0131 225 5006
E-mail: enquiries@couplescounselling.org

A counsellor or psychosexual doctor attached to your local **Family Planning Clinic** can help with sexual problems – address in your local phone book or ring the FPA's Helpline on 0845 310 1334.

Family Planning Association
2–12 Pentonville Road
London N1 9FP
Website: www.fpa.org.uk

The **British Association for Counselling** can suggest a counsellor in your area.

British Association for Counselling
1 Regent Place
Rugby
Warwickshire CV21 2PJ
Tel: 01788 550899
Website: www.counselling.co.uk
E-mail: bac@bac.co.uk

Asian Family Counselling Service offers counselling for members of the Asian community.

Asian Family Counselling Service
76 Church Road
Hanwell
London W7 1LB
Tel: 020 8567 5616
E-mail: afcs@hotmail.com

Jewish Marriage Council offers counselling for members of the Jewish Community.

Jewish Marriage Council
23 Ravenshurst Avenue
London NW4 4EE
Tel: 020 8203 6311
Website: www.jmc-uk.org
E-mail: info@jmc-uk.org

National Family Mediation can tell you of your nearest mediation centre.

National Family Mediation
9 Tavistock Place
London WC1H 9SN
Tel: 020 7383 5993
Website: www.nfm.u-net.com

In Scotland, **Family Mediation Scotland** can be reached on 0131 220 1610.

The National Council for the Divorced and Separated offer self-help groups and social events.

The National Council for the Divorced and Separated
168 Loxley Road
Malin Bridge
Sheffield S6 4TE
Lo-call Tel: 07041 478 120
Website: www.ncds.org.uk

Cruse Bereavement Care offers help for anyone grieving over a death. They have branches all over the country and can refer you to a local bereavement counsellor who can give face-to-face support.

Bereavement line: 0870 167 1677 (0845 758 5565 for Wales)
E-mail: info@crusebereavementcare.org.uk

Help with the family and children

ParentLine Plus gives support and telephone counselling to anyone in a parenting situation, whether you're married and whether or not the kids live with you full-time, whatever the worry or anxiety.

ParentLine Plus
Unit 520 Highgate Studios
53–79 Highgate Road
Kentish Town
London NW5 1TL
Freephone helpline: 0808 800 2222
Website: www.parentlineplus.org.uk

Kidscape can offer help with bullying and many other problems that young children might be experiencing.

Kidscape
2 Grosvenor Gardens
London SW1W 0DH
Tel: 020 7730 3300
E-mail: contact@kidscape.org.uk

Childline is for young people in need of support.
Freephone telephone number: 0800 1111
Childline Scotland has a dedicated bullying line on 0800 441111.

Website: www.childline.org.uk
E-mail: info@childline.org.uk

The **NSPCC** can help with sexual or any other type of child abuse. The Child Protection Helpline is a free, 24-hour service which provides counselling, information and advice for anyone concerned about a child at risk of abuse.

Tel: 0800 800 500
Website: www.nspcc.org.uk
E-mail: help@nspcc.org.uk

National Association of Child Contact Centres offers places where children can meet and play with the parent or other family members with whom they do not live, in a safe

and supervised environment. The child has the contact that
s/he needs with the missing parent while you have peace of
mind, knowing all of you are protected.

National Association of Child Contact Centres
Minerva House
Spaniel Row
Nottingham NG1 6EP
Tel: 0115 948 4557
Website: www.nacc.org.uk

Youth Access can give information about youth counselling
services.

Youth Access
1–2 Taylors Yard
67 Alderbrook Road
London SW12 8AD

The site is a website run by YouthNet UK that has an up-to-
date database on youth counselling services, accessed on the
internet.
Website: www.thesite.org.uk

One Parent Families has a wealth of information, advice
and support for parents on their own, from suggestions about
jobs and training, through rights and benefits, to child-care
and holidays.

One Parent Families
255 Kentish Town Road
London NW5 2LX
Helpline: 0800 018 5026
Website: www.oneparentfamilies.org.uk

Gingerbread run lone-parent self help groups
Tel: 0800 018 4318
Website: www.gingerbread.org.uk

The Daycare Trust can help with any aspect of child-care contact. Their hotline provides free information and advice for parents.

The Daycare Trust
Shoreditch Town Hall Annexe
380 Old Street
London EC1V 9LT
Tel: 020 7739 2866
Website: www.daycaretrust.org.uk

Drink and drugs

Drinkline can help with problems with drink or drugs.

Drinkline
Petersham House
57a Hatton Garden
London EC1N 8HP
Freephone: 0800 917 8282

Al-Anon helps anyone who has a family member with a drinking problem. **Alateen** are there to help the children of problem drinkers.

Al-Anon and Alateen
61 Great Dover Street
London SE1 4YF
Tel: 020 7403 0888 (24-hour confidential service)
Website: www.hexnet.co.uk/alanon

Adfam is the national charity for families and friends of drug users.

Adfam
Waterbridge House
32–36 Loman Street
London SE1 0EE
Tel: 020 7928 8900

Emotional or mental health

Mind can help with many emotional problems and have a range of leaflets on most of them.

Infoline: 0345 660163
For leaflets ring: 020 8510 2122

Saneline helps with any mental health problem from anorexia to schizophrenia.

Helpline: 08457 678 000
Website: mkn.co.uk/help/charity/sane/index
E-mail: sane@saneline.org.uk

The National Depression Campaign offers leaflets with suggestions of sources of help.

The National Depression Campaign
35 Westminster Bridge Road
London SE1 7JB
Tel: 020 7207 3293

Young Minds can help with worries over the emotional well-being of a child and suggests where you can get help, such as from the local Child and Family Health Consultative Services (Child Guidance Clinics) and local Youth Counselling and Information Services.

Helpline: 0800 018 2138
Tel: 020 7336 8445
Website: www.youngminds.org.uk

The Eating Disorders Association offers support and self-help to anyone suffering from anorexia, bulimia or any other eating disorder, or their families.

The Eating Disorders Association
1st Floor, Wensum House
103 Prince of Wales Road
Norwich
Norfolk NR1 1DW
Helpline: 01603 621 414
Youthline: 01603 765 050
E-mail: info@edauk.com

Help for the older person

SeniorLine is a free line run by Help the Aged, for all aspects
of advice for senior citizens, on 0800 650 065.

Domestic violence

Refuge offers help with any sort of domestic violence. It can
give you support and advice and tell you where to get help,
including somewhere safe to stay.
Refuge 24-hour national crisis line: 020 8995 4430

Women's Aid offers help with any sort of domestic violence.
It can give you support and advice and tell you where to get
help, including somewhere safe to stay.

Women's Aid
PO Box 391
Bristol BS99 7WS
National Helpline: 0345 023 468
E-mail: wafe@wafe.co.uk
Website: www.womensaid.org.uk

Victim Support can help anyone who has been affected by
violence, trauma or crime with counselling and support.

Helpline: 0845 303 0900

Practical Advice

Citizens' Advice Bureau for advice on any practical problems, such as worries about money, housing or legal matters. Address in the local phone book or at their website www.adviceguide.org.uk

The Solicitors Family Law Association can offer details of solicitors who practise a constructive and conciliatory approach to the legalities that follow a marriage breakdown.

The Solicitors Family Law Association
PO Box 302
Orpington
Kent BR6 8QX
Tel: 0345 586 671 (local rate) or 01689 850227

National Debtline for help with debt problems.
Tel: 0645 500 511

Libraries

A good place to look for other help is your local library. There is an enormous range of books and leaflets for any and every problem and situation. If you ask the librarian, they will be able to come up with something that could help. Your local library is the place to find out about self-help groups, social clubs and activities. If you're lonely and/or bored or need a new direction or advice on training, go and ask what's on offer.

And finally . . .

If you feel desparate and alone, please don't forget that the **Samaritans** are at the end of a phone line at all times. The number you can call at any time, from any phone for the price of a local call, is 08457 909 090, or ask the operator to put you through. Or find them online at www.samaritans.org.uk or e-mail jo@samaritans.org

INDEX